GENERAL PRACTICE IN NEW YORK

Volume 23

By

ROBERT L. OSTERTAG
HON. JAMES D. BENSON

Sections 21.1 to 27.58

1999 Pocket Part

Insert this Pocket Part in back of Volume

ST. PAUL, MINN.
WEST GROUP
1999

GENERAL PRACTICE IN NEW YORK
FORMS ON DISK™

The **Forms on Disk™** which accompany these volumes provide instant access to WordPerfect 5.1/5.2 versions of the forms included in *General Practice in New York*. These electronic forms will save you hours of time drafting legal documents. The electronic forms can be loaded into your word processing software and formatted to match the document style of your law firm. These electronic forms become templates for you to use over and over without having to retype them each time.

The forms in Volumes 20, 21, 22, 23, 24 and 25 that are included on the accompanying disks are marked with the following disk icon for easy identification.

COPYRIGHT © 1999
By
WEST GROUP

This is the 1999 Pocket Part to Volume 23 of WEST'S NEW YORK PRACTICE SERIES

West's New York Practice Series

Vol. 1	Walker, et al., New York Limited Liability Companies and Partnerships: A Guide to Law and Practice
Vols. 2-4	Haig, et al., Commercial Litigation in New York State Courts
Vol. 5	Barker and Alexander, Evidence in New York State and Federal Courts
Vol. 6	Greenberg, Marcus, et al., New York Criminal Law
Vol. 7	Marks, et al., New York Pretrial Criminal Procedure
Vol. 8	Davies, Stecich, Gold, et al., New York Civil Appellate Practice
Vol. 9	Ginsberg, Weinberg, et al., Environmental Law and Regulation in New York
Vol. 10	Sobie, et al., New York Family Court Practice
Vols. 11-12	Scheinkman, et al., New York Law of Domestic Relation

Vol. 13	Taber, et al., Employment Litigation in New York
Vols. 14-16	Kreindler, Rodriguez, et al., New York Law of Torts
Vols. 17-19	Field, Moskin, et al., New York and Delaware Business Organizations: Choice, Formation, Operation, Financing and Acquisitions
Vols. 20-25	Ostertag, Benson, et al., General Practice in New York
Vol. 26	Borchers, Markell, et al., New York State Administrative Procedure and Practice
Vol. A	Borges, et al., Enforcing Judgments and Collecting Debts in New York
Vols. B-C	Bensel, Frank, McKeon, et al., Personal Injury Practice in New York
Vols. D-E	Preminger, et al., Trusts and Estates Practice in New York
Vols. F-G	Finkelstein and Ferrara, Landlord and Tenant Practice in New York

FOREWORD

Here is the first update to *General Practice in New York*, volume 23 of the New York Practice Series. The pocket part covers the significant changes in the applicable law from publication of the original volume until 1999. Many of the updates were prepared by one or more of the original chapter authors; others were editorially prepared in-house by West and are so indicated. With respect to chapters of the book not updated at all, West makes no representations with respect to the current status of ther material therein.

December 1999

COORDINATED RESEARCH IN NEW YORK FROM WEST

New York Practice 2d
David D. Siegel

Handling the DWI Case in New York
Peter Gerstenzang

New York Elder Law Practice
Vincent J. Russo and Marvin Rachlin

WEST'S McKINNEY'S FORMS

Civil Practice Law and Rules

Uniform Commercial Code

Business Corporation Law

Matrimonial and Family Law

Real Property Practice

Estates and Surrogate Practice

Criminal Procedure Law

Not-For-Profit Corporation Law

Tax Practice and Procedure

Local Government Forms

Selected Consolidated Law Forms

McKinney's Consolidated Laws of New York Annotated

West's New York Legal Update

New York Digest

New York Law Finder

PAMPHLETS

New York Civil Practice Law and Rules

New York Sentence Charts

Westlaw®

COORDINATED RESEARCH FROM WEST GROUP

WEST*Check*® and WESTMATE®

West CD–ROM Libraries™

To order any of these New York practice tools, call your West Group Representative or 1–800–328–9352.

> **NEED RESEARCH HELP?**
>
> **If you have research questions concerning Westlaw or West Group Publications, call West Group's Reference Attorneys at 1–800–733–2889.**

WESTLAW® ELECTRONIC RESEARCH GUIDE

Coordinating Legal Research with Westlaw

The *New York Practice Series* is an essential aid to legal research. Westlaw provides a vast, online library of over 8000 collections of documents and services that can supplement research begun in this publication, encompassing:

- Federal and state primary law (statutes, regulations, rules, and case law), including West's editorial enhancements, such as headnotes, Key Number classifications, annotations

- Secondary law resources (texts and treatises published by West Group and by other publishers, as well as law reviews)

- Legal news

- Directories of attorneys and experts

- Court records and filings

- Citators

Specialized topical subsets of these resources have been created for more than thirty areas of practice.

In addition to legal information, there are general news and reference databases and a broad array of specialized materials frequently useful in connection with legal matters, covering accounting, business, environment, ethics, finance, medicine, social and physical sciences.

This guide will focus on a few aspects of Westlaw use to supplement research begun in this publication, and will direct you to additional sources of assistance.

Databases

A database is a collection of documents with some features in common. It may contain statutes, court decisions, administrative materials, commentaries, news or other information. Each database has a unique identifier, used in many Westlaw commands to select a database of interest. For example, the database containing New York cases has the identifier NY-CS.

The Westlaw Directory is a comprehensive list of databases with information about each database, including the types of documents each contains. The first page of a standard or customized Westlaw Directory is displayed upon signing on to Westlaw, except when prior, saved research is resumed. To access the Westlaw Directory at any time, enter DB.

Databases of potential interest in connection with your research include:

NY-AG	New York Attorney General Opinions
NYETH-EO	New York Ethics Opinions
NYETH-CS	Legal Ethics & Professional Responsibility - New York Cases
WLD-NY	West's Legal Directory - New York
LAWPRAC	The Legal Practice Database

For information as to currentness and search tips regarding any Westlaw database, enter the SCOPE command SC followed by the database identifier (e.g., SC NY-CS). It is not necessary to include the identifier to obtain scope information about the currently selected database.

Westlaw Highlights

Use of this publication may be supplemented through the Westlaw Bulletin (WLB), the Westlaw New York State Bulletin (WSB-NY) and various Topical Highlights. Highlights databases contain summaries of significant judicial, legislative and administrative developments and are updated daily; they are searchable both from an automatic list of recent documents and using general Westlaw search methods for documents accumulated over time. The full text of any judicial decision may be retrieved by entering FIND.

Consult the Westlaw Directory (enter DB) for a complete, current listing of highlights databases.

Retrieving a Specific Case

The FIND command can be used to quickly retrieve a case whose citation is known. For example:

FI 616 A.2d 1336

Updating Case Law Research

There are a variety of citator services on Westlaw for use in updating research.

KeyCite℠ is an enhanced citator service that integrates all the case law on Westlaw. KeyCite provides direct and negative indirect history for any case within the scope of its coverage, citations to other decisions and secondary materials on Westlaw that have mentioned or discussed the cited case, and a complete integration with West Group's Key Number System so that you can track a legal issue explored in a case. KeyCite is as current as Westlaw and includes all cases on Westlaw, including unpublished opinions. To view the KeyCite history of a displayed case, enter the command KC. To view the KeyCite information for a selected case, simply enter a command in the following form:

KC 113 SCT 2786

To see a complete list of publications covered by KeyCite, enter the command KC PUBS. To ascertain the scope of coverage, enter the command SC KC. For the complete list of commands available enter KC CMDS.

Retrieving Statutes, Court Rules and Regulations

Annotated and unannotated versions of the New York statutes are searchable on Westlaw (identifiers NY-ST-ANN and NY-ST), as are New York court rules (NY-RULES) and New York Administrative Code (NY-ADC).

The United States Code and United States Code - Annotated are searchable databases on Westlaw (identifiers USC and USCA, respectively), as are federal court rules (US-RULES) and regulations (CFR).

In addition, the FIND command may be used to retrieve specific provisions by citation, obviating the need for database selection or search. To FIND a desired document, enter FI, followed by the citation of the desired document, using the full name of the publication, or one of the abbreviated styles recognized by Westlaw.

If Westlaw does not recognize the style you enter, you may enter one of the following, using US, NY, or any other state code in place of XX:

FI XX-ST	Displays templates for codified statutes
FI XX-LEGIS	Displays templates for legislation
FI XX-RULES	Displays templates for rules
FI XX-ORDERS	Displays templates for court orders

Alternatively, entering FI followed by the publication's full name or an accepted abbreviation will normally display templates, useful jump possibilities, or helpful information necessary to complete the FIND process. For example:

FI USCA	Displays templates for United States Code - Annotated
FI FRAP	Displays templates for Federal Rules of Appellate Procedure
FI FRCP	Displays templates for Federal Rules of Civil Procedure
FI FRCRP	Displays templates for Federal Rules of Criminal Procedure
FI FRE	Displays templates for Federal Rules of Evidence
FI CFR	Displays templates for Code of Federal Regulations
FI FR	Displays templates for Federal Register

To view the complete list of FINDable documents and associated prescribed forms, enter FI PUBS.

WESTLAW ELECTRONIC RESEARCH GUIDE

Updating Research in re Statutes, Rules and Regulations

When viewing a statute, rule or regulation on Westlaw after a search or FIND command, it is easy to update your research. A message will appear on the screen if relevant amendments, repeals or other new material are available through the UPDATE feature. Entering the UPDATE command will display such material.

Documents used to update New York statutes are also searchable in New York Legislative Service (NY-LEGIS). Those used to update rules are searchable in New York Orders (NY-ORDERS).

Documents used to update federal statutes, rules, and regulations are searchable in the United States Public Laws (US-PL), Federal Orders (US-ORDERS) and Federal Register (FR) databases, respectively.

When documents citing a statute, rule or regulation are of interest, Shepard's Citations on Westlaw may be of assistance. That service covers federal constitutional provisions, statutes and administrative provisions, and corresponding materials from many states. The command SH PUBS displays a directory of publications which may be Shepardized on Westlaw. Consult the Westlaw manual for more information about citator services.

Using Westlaw as a Citator

For research beyond the coverage of any citator service, go directly to the databases (cases, for example) containing citing documents and use standard Westlaw search techniques to retrieve documents citing specific constitutional provisions, statutes, standard jury instructions or other authorities.

Fortunately, the specific portion of a citation is often reasonably distinctive, such as 22:636.1, 301.65, 401(k), 12-21-5, 12052. When it is, a search on that specific portion alone may retrieve applicable documents without any substantial number of inapplicable ones (unless the number happens to be coincidentally popular in another context).

Similarly, if the citation involves more than one number, such as 42 U.S.C.A. §1201, a search containing both numbers (e.g., 42 +5 1201) is likely to produce mostly desired information, even though the component numbers are common.

If necessary, the search may be limited in several ways:

A. Switch from a general database to one containing mostly cases within the subject area of the cite being researched;

WESTLAW ELECTRONIC RESEARCH GUIDE

B. Use a connector (&, /S, /P, etc.) to narrow the search to documents including terms which are highly likely to accompany the correct citation in the context of the issue being researched;

C. Include other citation information in the query. Because of the variety of citation formats used in documents, this option should be used primarily where other options prove insufficient. Below are illustrative queries for any database containing New York cases:

N.Y.Const.! Const.! Constitution /s 6 VI +3 3

will retrieve cases citing the New York State Constitution, Art. 6, §3; and

"Criminal Procedure Law" CPL /s 30.30

will retrieve cases citing Criminal Procedure Law §30.30.

Alternative Retrieval Methods

WIN® (Westlaw Is Natural™) allows you to frame your issue in plain English to retrieve documents:

Does new trial motion extend (toll) the time for filing (taking) appeal?

Alternatively, retrieval may be focused by use of the Terms and Connectors method:

TO(30) /P DI(NEW +1 TRIAL /P EXTEND! EXTENSION TOLL! /P APPEAL)

In databases with Key Numbers, either of the above examples will identify Appeal and Error ⇐345.1 as a Key Number collecting headnotes relevant to this issue if there are pertinent cases.

Since the Key Numbers are affixed to points of law by trained specialists based on conceptual understanding of the case, relevant cases that were not retrieved by either of the language-dependent methods will often be found at a Key Number.

Similarly, citations in retrieved documents (to cases, statutes, rules, etc.) may suggest additional, fruitful research using other Westlaw databases (e.g., annotated statutes, rules) or services (e.g., citator services).

Key Number Search

Frequently, case law research rapidly converges on a few topics, headings and Key Numbers within West's Key Number System that are likely to contain relevant cases. These may be discovered from known, relevant reported cases from any jurisdiction; Library References in West publications; browsing in a digest; or browsing the Key Number System on Westlaw using the JUMP feature or the KEY command.

WESTLAW ELECTRONIC RESEARCH GUIDE

Once discovered, topics, subheadings or Key Numbers are useful as search terms (in databases containing reported cases) alone or with other search terms, to focus the search within a narrow range of potentially relevant material.

For example, to retrieve cases with at least one headnote classified to Appeal and Error ⇛345.1, sign on to a caselaw database and enter

    30k345.1   [use with other search terms, if desired]

The topic name (Appeal and Error) is replaced by its numerical equivalent (30) and the ⇛ by the letter k. A list of topics and their numerical equivalents is in the Westlaw Reference Manual and is displayed in Westlaw when the KEY command is entered.

Using JUMP

Westlaw's JUMP feature allows you to move from one document to another or from one part of a document to another, then easily return to your original place, without losing your original result. Opportunities to move in this manner are marked in the text with a JUMP symbol (▶). Whenever you see the JUMP symbol, you may move to the place designated by the adjacent reference by using the Tab, arrow keys or mouse click to position the cursor on the JUMP symbol, then pressing Enter or clicking again with the mouse.

Within the text of a court opinion, JUMP arrows are adjacent to case cites and federal statute cites, and adjacent to parenthesized numbers marking discussions corresponding to headnotes.

On a screen containing the text of a headnote, the JUMP arrows allow movement to the corresponding discussion in the text of the opinion,

  ▶ (3)

and allow browsing West's Key Number System beginning at various heading levels:

- ▶ 30   APPEAL AND ERROR
- ▶ 30VII   Transfer of Cause
- ▶ 30VII(A)   Time of Taking Proceedings
- ▶ 30k343   Commencement of Period of Limitation
- ▶ 30k345.1 k. Motion for new trial.

To return from a JUMP, enter GB (except for JUMPs between a headnote and the corresponding discussion in opinion, for which there is a matching number in parenthesis in both headnote and opinion). Returns from successive JUMPs (e.g., from case to cited case to case cited by cited case) without intervening returns may be accomplished by repeated entry of GB or by using the MAP command.

WESTLAW ELECTRONIC RESEARCH GUIDE

General Information

The information provided above illustrates some of the ways Westlaw can complement research using this publication. However, this brief overview illustrates only some of the power of Westlaw. The full range of Westlaw search techniques is available to support your research.

Please consult the Westlaw Reference Manual for additional information or assistance or call West's Reference Attorneys at 1-800-REF-ATTY (1-800-733-2889).

For information about subscribing to Westlaw, please call 1-800-328-9352.

SUMMARY OF CONTENTS

Volume 20

Chapter		Page
1.	Business Organizations: Corporations	2
2.	Non-corporate Entities	16
3.	Municipal Law	19
4.	Municipal Law	21
6.	Buying and Selling a Small Business	25

Volume 21

7.	Consumer Law	2
8.	Enforcement of Money Judgments	4
9.	Bankruptcy	5
11.	Mortgage Foreclosure	11
12.	Purchase and Sale of Real Estate	25

Volume 22

14.	Eminent Domain	2
15.	Environmental Law	5
16.	Land Use Law	8
17.	Employment Law	14
18.	Civil Rights Law	16
19.	Immigration and Nationality Law Permanent Residence Applications	39
20.	Adoptions	52

Volume 23

21.	Domestic Relations	2
22.	Guardianship	9
23.	Elder Law	21
24.	Estate Planning	30
25.	Probate and Estate Administration	37
26.	Personal Injury	51

Volume 24

28.	Legal Malpractice	2
29.	Medical Malpractice	20
30.	Damages	21

XVII

SUMMARY OF CONTENTS

Chapter	**Page**
31. Insurance	31
32. Workers' Compensation	34
33. Local Criminal Court Practice	39
34. Social Security Disability Cases	50
35. Income Tax	55
37. Civil Appellate Practice Before the Appellate Division and Other Intermediate Appellate Courts	58

Volume 25

38. Criminal Appellate Practice Before the Appellate Division and Other Intermediate Appellate Courts | 2
39. Civil and Criminal Appeals to the Court of Appeals | 4

Table of Statutes | 5
Table of Rules and Regulations | 15
Table of Cases | 17
Index | 31

XVIII

WEST'S
NEW YORK PRACTICE
SERIES

General Practice in New York

Volume 23

Chapter 21

DOMESTIC RELATIONS

(update prepared in-house)

Table of Sections

21.5	Jurisdiction—Uniform Child Custody Jurisdiction Act
21.19	Grounds for Divorce—No Official No–Fault Ground
21.20	___ Cruel and Inhuman Treatment
21.21	___ Cruel and Inhuman Treatment—Defenses
21.22	___ Abandonment
21.30	___ Divorce Action Based Upon Living Apart Pursuant to Separation Agreement
21.37	Equitable Distribution—Characterization of Property—Marital Property
21.39	___ Classification of Property—Marital Property—Professional Practices, Licenses, Degrees and Careers
21.49	Maintenance—Current Trends
21.51	___ Tax Consequences
21.53	Child Support—Child Support Standards Act
21.54	___ Child Support Standards Act—Where Statutory Percentages Are Unfair or Inappropriate
21.55	___ Child Support Standards Act
21.65	Net Worth Statement
21.69	Modification—Maintenance
21.70	___ Child Support
21.72	Enforcement
21.76	Practice Considerations—Procedure for Attorneys in Domestic Relations Matters
21.79	___ Rules Regarding Case Management
21.80	Procedural Checklist—Calendar Control

Westlaw Electronic Research

See Westlaw Electronic Research Guide preceding the Summary of Contents.

§ 21.5 Jurisdiction—Uniform Child Custody Jurisdiction Act

PAGE 10:

[*Add to end of note 1.*]

1. *See* Matter of Kathleen S., N.Y.L.J., 4/30/98, p. 31, col. 6 (after the child's home state of Florida declined jurisdiction, a New York family court took the case, reasoning that it was not in the child's best interest to deny the parents any forum).

PAGE 11:

[*Add to end of note 6.*]

6. *See, e.g.,* Curtis v. Curtis, 237 A.D.2d 984, 984, 654 N.Y.S.2d 538, 539 (4th Dept. 1997) (court refused to consider arguments by a mother that a New York court was an inconvenient forum since she had previously removed her child to Virginia in violation of a New York court order).

§ 21.19 Grounds for Divorce—No Official No–Fault Ground

PAGE 20:

[*Add to end of note 1.*]

1. *See* Van Vlack v. Van Vlack, 233 A.D.2d 895, 895, 649 N.Y.S.2d 255, 256 (4th Dept.1996) (case of divorce on grounds of cruel and inhuman treatment; held that the same standard of proof that governs actions for divorce is required in actions for separation).

§ 21.20 Grounds for Divorce—Cruel and Inhuman Treatment

PAGE 20:

[*Add to end of note 1.*]

1. *See* M.M. v. E.M., 248 A.D.2d 109, 111, 669 N.Y.S.2d 543, 544 (1st Dept.1998) (court held as legally sufficient a claim by the plaintiff that during a two-year period, the defendant was regularly intoxicated and continually berated, ridiculed, and verbally abused plaintiff, his family, and his profession); Wilson v. Wilson, 244 A.D.2d 646, 647, 663 N.Y.S.2d 710, 711 (3d Dept. 1997) (divorce complaint dismissed because plaintiff failed to allege how the conduct at issue endangered her physical or mental well-being and made it unsafe or improper for plaintiff to live with defendant, and also did not provide a sufficient connection between defendant's alleged acts and the plaintiff's well being).

§ 21.21 Grounds for Divorce—Cruel and Inhuman Treatment—Defenses

PAGE 23:

[*Add to end of note 1.*]

1. *But see* Nabi v. Nabi, 242 A.D.2d 870, 870, 662 N.Y.S.2d 906, 907 (N.Y.A.D. 4th Dept.1997) (evidence of acts of cruel and inhuman treatment occurring more than five years before the date of the commencement of the action may be used to prove a continuous course of conduct, provided that at least one cruel or inhuman act occurred during the statutory period).

§ 21.22 Grounds for Divorce—Abandonment

PAGE 25:

[*Add to end of note 8.*]

8. *See also* Tissot v. Tissot, 243 A.D.2d 462, 463, 662 N.Y.S.2d 599, 600 (2d Dept. 1997) (constructive abandonment occurs when a spouse refuses to engage in sexual relations for one or more years and such a refusal is continued, unjustified, and willful).

§ 21.30 Grounds for Divorce—Divorce Action Based Upon Living Apart Pursuant to Separation Agreement

PAGE 32:

[*Add to end of note 4.*]

4. *See* Matisoff v. Dobi, 90 N.Y.2d 127, 138, 659 N.Y.S.2d 209, 215, 681 N.E.2d 376, 382 (1997) (holding that an unacknowledged separation agreement was unenforceable but suggesting that equitable factors, such as who requested the agreement, the parties' conduct pursuant to it, and the admission of signature, would be considered in a judicial resolution of the martial issues); Arizin v. Covello, 175 Misc.2d 453, 457, 669 N.Y.S.2d 189, 192 (Sup.Ct.N.Y.Co. 1998) (court held that unacknowledged nuptial agreement which is acknowledged on subsequent date is enforceable as long as subsequent acknowledgment complies with statutory requirements; distinguished *Rose* as in that case there was no subsequent acknowledgment).

§ 21.37 Equitable Distribution—Characterization of Property—Marital Property

PAGE 39:

[*Add to end of note 1.*]

1. *See* DeJesus v. DeJesus, 90 N.Y.2d 643, 652, 665 N.Y.S.2d 36, 41, 687 N.E.2d 1319, 1324 (1997) (court held that restricted stock plan interests are marital property to the extent that such interests were granted in recognition of the employee's services until the date of the commencement of the divorce action, but such interests are not marital property to the extent they represent incentives for future services; court determined which portion of the stock plan interests constituted marital property and equitably distributed that part, but left alone the portion of the interests which were incentives for post-divorce services as separate property not to be equitably distributed).

§ 21.39 Equitable Distribution—Classification of Property—Marital Property—Professional Practices, Licenses, Degrees and Careers

PAGE 44:

[*Add to note 14.*]

14. Note that in Bystricky v. Bystricky, 177 Misc.2d 914, 677 N.Y.S.2d 443 (Sup. Ct. Nassau Cty., 1998), the court declined to follow the reasoning of Elkus v. Elkus.

§ 21.49 Maintenance—Current Trends

PAGE 62:

[*Add year to 2nd citation.. It is to read as follows...*]

6. ...; McLane v. McLane, 209 A.D.2d 1001, 619 N.Y.S.2d 899 (4th Dep't 1994), ...

§ 21.51 Maintenance—Tax Consequences
PAGE 63:

[*In note 1, change reference from 26 U.S.C.A. § 71(a) to*]

1. 26 U.S.C.A. § 71(b).

§ 21.53 Child Support—Child Support Standards Act
PAGE 66:

[*Add to note 1.*]

1. *See* Isaacs v. Isaacs, 246 A.D.2d 428, 667 N.Y.S.2d 740 (1st Dept.1998). (trial court properly imputed income to the husband based upon cash and other benefits he received from his family controlled company when the husband could manipulate the finances of the company and the husband's reported income declined drastically immediately after the wife filed the action).

§ 21.54 Child Support—Child Support Standards Act—Where Statutory Percentages Are Unfair or Inappropriate
PAGE 68:

[*Delete "and" preceding "(9) provided..." and insert the following between "custodial parent" and footnote 3.*]

; and (10) other factors relevant in each case.

§ 21.55 Child Support—Child Support Standards Act
PAGE 70:

[*Add the following as the second-to-last paragraph on page 70:*]

Lower courts have remained uncertain about when the Family Ct. Act § 413(1)(f) formula should be applied to income over $80,000 per annum. Third Department courts have interpreted *Cassano* as establishing a presumption that the statutory formula should be used for income over $80,000. *See* Jones v. Reese, 227 A.D.2d 783, 642 N.Y.S.2d 378 (3d Dept.1996) (sustaining the application of the formula to combined parental income of over $315,000). Second Department courts have been more reluctant to consider a presumption of applicability of the statutory formula to income over $80,000. *See* Straker v. Straker, 219 A.D.2d 707, 631 N.Y.S.2d 767 (2d Dept.1995) (holding it was proper to limit the formula to the first $80,000 of income); Zaremba v. Zaremba, 222 A.D.2d 500, 635 N.Y.S.2d 532 (2d Dept..1995) (holding that before the formula can be applied by trial courts, the courts must set forth the factors considered and the reasons for the ultimate determination). *See also* Niagara County Dept. of Social Services on Behalf of D.A.H. v. C.B., 234 A.D.2d 897, 899, 651 N.Y.S.2d 785, 787 (4th Dept.1996) ("the blind application of the statutory formula to the parties' combined aggregate income over $80,000, without any express findings or record evidence of the children's actual needs, constitutes an abdication of judicial responsi-

§ 21.55   DOMESTIC RELATIONS   Ch. 21

bility and renders meaningless the statutory provision setting a cap on strict application of the formula", quoting Matter of Panossian v. Panossian, 201 A.D.2d 983, 607 N.Y.S.2d 840 (4th Dept.1994)).

§ 21.65   Net Worth Statement
PAGE 80:

[*Add to note 4.*]

4. In addition, a party making fraudulent or deceitful statements in a net worth statement may be punished for contempt of court. See Kim v. Kim, 170 Misc.2d 968, 971, 652 N.Y.S.2d 694, 696 (Sup.Ct. Suffolk County, 1996) (court imposed $10,000 fine on husband for making fraudulent disclosures).

§ 21.69   Modification—Maintenance
PAGE 83:

[*Replace the quotation in the last sentence of this section because the printed one is slightly inaccurate.*]

"no modification of a prior order or judgment incorporating the terms of said agreement shall be made as to maintenance without a showing of extreme hardship on either party, in which event the judgment or order as modified shall supersede the terms of the prior agreement and judgment for such period of time and under such circumstances as the court determines."

§ 21.70   Modification—Child Support
PAGE 83:

[*Replace note 3 with the following.*]

3. DRL § 240(1)(h) provides:

Upon the application of either parent, or of any other person or party having the care, custody and control of such child pursuant to such judgment or order, after such notice to the other party, parties or persons having such care, custody and control and given in such manner as the court shall direct, the court may annul or modify any such direction, whether made by order or final judgment, or in case no such direction shall have been made in the final judgment may, with respect to any judgment of annulment or declaring the nullity of a void marriage rendered on or after September first, nineteen hundred forty, or any judgment of separation or divorce whenever rendered, amend the judgment by inserting such direction.

[*The last paragraph on p. 83 should read as follows.*]

The Child Support Standards Act (Domestic Relations Law Section 240(1–b)) provides that in any action or proceeding for modification of an order of child support existing prior to the effective date of the 1997 amendment, the child support standards set forth in the Act do not constitute a change of circumstances warranting modification of such support order; provided, however, that (1) where the circumstances warrant modification of such order, or (2) where any party objects to an adjusted child support order made or proposed at the direction of the support collection unit pursuant to Section 111–h or Section 111–n of the Social Services Law, and the court is reviewing the current order of child support, such standards shall be applied by the court in its determination with regard to the request for modification, or disposition of an objection to an adjusted child support order made or proposed by a support collection unit.[4] In applying such standards, when the order to be modified incorporates by reference or merges with a validly executed separation agreement or stipulation of settlement, the court may consider, in addition to the factors set forth in paragraph (f) of Section 240, the provisions of such agreement or stipulation concerning property distribution, distributive award and/or maintenance in determining whether the amount calculated by using the standards would be unjust or inappropriate.[5]

4. DRL § 240(1–b)(b)(1).
5. Id.

[*The first sentence of the second full paragraph on p. 84 should read as follows.*]

Any order of support issued on behalf of a child in receipt of family assistance or child support enforcement services pursuant to section one hundred eleven-g of the social services law shall be subject to review and adjustment by the support collection unit pursuant to section one hundred eleven-n of the social services law.[7]

7. DRL § 240 (2)(c).

[*The third sentence of the paragraph and accompanying footnote should be deleted. It begins:*]

All court orders directing...

§ 21.72 Enforcement

PAGE 86:

[*Replace note 1 with the following.*]

1. DRL § 236(B)(9)(a) provides:
All orders or judgments entered in matrimonial actions shall be enforceable pursuant to section fifty-two hundred forty-one or fifty-two hundred forty-two of the civil practice law and rules, or in any other manner provided by law. Orders or judgments for child support, alimony and maintenance shall also be enforceable pursuant to article fifty-two of the civil practice law and rules upon a debtor's default as such term is defined in paragraph seven of subdivision (a) of section fifty-two hundred forty-one of the civil practice law and rules. The establishment of a default shall be subject to the procedures established for the determination of a mistake of fact for income executions pursuant to subdivision (e) of section fifty-two hundred forty-one of the civil practice law and rules. For the purposes of enforcement of child support orders or combined spousal and child support orders pursuant to section five thousand two hundred forty-one of the civil practice law and rules, a "default" shall be deemed to include amounts arising from retroactive support. The court may, and if a party shall fail or refuse to pay maintenance, distributive award or child support the court shall, upon notice and an opportunity to the defaulting party to be heard, require the party to furnish a surety, or the sequestering and sale of assets for the purpose of enforcing any award for maintenance, distributive award or child support and for the payment of reasonable and necessary attorney's fees and disbursements.

§ 21.76 Practice Considerations—Procedure for Attorneys in Domestic Relations Matters

PAGE 91:

[*Delete second full paragraph ("A closing statement ... telephone number and signature.") and all accompanying footnotes. 22 NYCRR § 1400.6 was repealed (filed Feb. 24, 1997, effective March 1, 1997).*]

§ 21.79 Practice Considerations—Rules Regarding Case Management

PAGE 95:

[*First three lines on page ("Each attorney ... retainer agreement") and accompanying footnote should be deleted. 22 NYCRR § 202.16(c)(3) has been removed from the code. Footnote 10, the "Practice Pointer," should be deleted. The May 1, 1996 amendment has been removed from (e).*]

[*First sentence of last paragraph should read: "A preliminary conference is to be ordered by the court to be held within 45 days after the action has been assigned." Footnote 11 remains unchanged.*]

PAGE 97:

[*In the second paragraph, both references to "20 days" should be removed and replaced with "30 days."*]

§ 21.80 Procedural Checklist—Calendar Control

PAGE 99:

[*Paragraph "3." and corresponding footnote should be deleted. In the paragraph numbered "5.", "30 days" should be replaced by "45 days". In the paragraph numbered "8.", the term "20 days" in the first sentence should be replaced by "30 days".*]

Chapter 22

GUARDIANSHIP

by
Miriam R. Adelman

Table of Sections

22.2	Strategy
22.8	Legislative Purpose of Mental Hygiene Law Article 81
22.12	Power to Appoint Guardian—Elements
22.13	____ Incapacity
22.14	____ Primary Considerations
22.15	____ Jurisdiction
22.16	____ Venue
22.17	____ Standing to Commence Proceeding
22.20	Proceeding to Appoint Guardian—Time and Method of Service of Notice
22.27	Court Evaluator—Compensation
22.28	____ Appointment of Counsel for the Alleged Incompetent Person
22.31	Hearing and Order—Procedure
22.32	____ Presence of Person Alleged to be Incapacitated
22.33	____ Evidence
22.35	____ Findings of the Court—Voluntary Appointment
22.38	____ Dispositional Alternatives
22.39	____ Award of Counsel Fees to Petitioner
22.41	____ Person to Be Appointed Guardian—Priority and Criteria for Appointment
22.47	Role of Guardian—Powers; Property Management
22.48	____ Substituted Judgment
22.53	____ Powers; Personal Needs
22.54	____ Effect of Appointment on Incapacitated Person
22.61	Compensation of Guardian
22.69	Removal, Discharge and Resignation of Guardian—Removal
22.70	____ Discharge or Modification of Powers

Westlaw Electronic Research
See Westlaw Electronic Research Guide preceding the Summary of Contents.

---

§ 22.2 Strategy

PAGE 169:

[*Add to note 9.*]

9. *Cf.*, Matter of Seidner, N.Y.L.J., 10/8/97, p. 28, col. 4 (Sup. Ct., Nassau County) (Medical evidence was excluded after objection by attorney for AIP, relying on privilege provisions of Civil Practice Law and Rules § 4504. The mere fact that a

§ 22.2 GUARDIANSHIP Ch. 22

party is forced to defend an action does not permit an inference of waiver by conduct, and the party's simple denial of allegations of such an action does not constitute any affirmative assertion of his condition. While the AIP vehemently opposed the appointment of a guardian for himself, nowhere in his testimony or in his interview by the court evaluator did he discuss or refer to his mental condition, thus there was no waiver of the privilege.)

§ 22.8 Legislative Purpose of Mental Hygiene Law Article 81

PAGE 185:

4. Matter of Maher, cited in Footnote 4, *appeal denied*, 86 N.Y.2d 703, 631 N.Y.S.2d 607, 655 N.E.2d 704 (1995), *reconsideration denied*, 86 N.Y.2d 886, 635 N.Y.S.2d 951, 659 N.E.2d 774 (1995).

[Add at end of second paragraph in note 4.]

4. See Matter of Addo, N.Y.L.J., 9/30/97, p. 26, col. 4 (Sup. Ct., Bronx County) (Where the infant was not expected to reach competence upon reaching majority, the court directed that the settlement funds be held under Mental Hygiene Law Article 81 to insure maximum protection. Civil Practice Law and Rules Article 12 is the usual vehicle for holding the proceeds of an infant's personal injury settlement until the infant reaches majority. The purpose of Mental Hygiene Law Article 81 was to create a guardianship law to meet the needs of an incapacitated or disabled elderly person and does not address the circumstances where the incapacitated person is an infant. While the statute does not preclude use for the young, the statute is silent with respect to the parental obligations and responsibilities to provide support for the incapacitated child. Only in the case where the infant is not expected to reach competence upon attaining majority are funds held under Mental Hygiene Law Article 81 to insure maximum protection. However, Mental Hygiene Law Article 81 does not diminish the principle that a child is entitled to parental support. Therefore, case law developed under Civil Practice Law and Rules Article 12 governs an application under Mental Hygiene Law Article 81 to withdraw infant funds.)

PAGE 186:

5. Matter of Maher, cited in Footnote 5, *appeal denied*, 86 N.Y.2d 703, 631 N.Y.S.2d 607, 655 N.E.2d 704 (1995), *reconsideration denied*, 86 N.Y.2d 886, 635 N.Y.S.2d 951, 659 N.E.2d 774 (1995).

[Add to note 9.]

9. See Matter of Estate of Bernice B., 176 Misc.2d 550, 672 N.Y.S.2d 994 (Surr. Ct., N.Y. County, 1998) (A party to a probate proceeding in Surrogate's Court, determined to be incapacitated and for whom a guardian *ad litem* had been appointed could not be bound by such guardian's consent to a settlement, over such party's objections. Notwithstanding the determination of incapacity for the purposes of appointing a guardian *ad litem*, such party retains the right to be heard in person as a party to the proceeding, including the right to veto a settlement, unless and until she has been adjudicated an "incapacitated person" pursuant to the provisions of Mental Hygiene Law Article 81.)

§ 22.12 Power to Appoint Guardian—Elements

PAGE 190:

1. Matter of Maher, cited in Footnote 1, *appeal denied*, 86 N.Y.2d 703, 631 N.Y.S.2d 607, 655 N.E.2d 704 (1995), *reconsideration denied*, 86 N.Y.2d 886, 635 N.Y.S.2d 951, 659 N.E.2d 774 (1995).

5. Matter of Maher, cited in Footnote 5, *appeal denied*, 86 N.Y.2d 703, 631 N.Y.S.2d 607, 655 N.E.2d 704 (1995), *reconsideration*

denied, 86 N.Y.2d 886, 635 N.Y.S.2d 951, 659 N.E.2d 774 (1995).

§ 22.13 Power to Appoint Guardian—Incapacity

PAGE 191:

1. Matter of Maher, cited in Footnote 1, *appeal denied*, 86 N.Y.2d 703, 631 N.Y.S.2d 607, 655 N.E.2d 704 (1995), *reconsideration denied*, 86 N.Y.2d 886, 635 N.Y.S.2d 951, 659 N.E.2d 774 (1995).

[Add to note 6.]

6. See Matter of New York Presbyterian Hospital (J.H.L.), N.Y.L.J., 6/4/99, p. 33, col. 4 (Sup. Ct., Westchester County) (The finding in a Mental Hygiene Law Article 81 proceeding that a person is incapacitated does not, as a matter of law, deprive such person of the right to a hearing pursuant to Mental Hygiene Law Article 33 (*Rivers Hearing*) on the issue of whether she should be forcibly medicated. Appointment of a Mental Hygiene Law Article 81 guardian does not deprive a person of the right to refuse a course of treatment, including the forcible administration of psychotropic medications. There is no presumption that such individuals are incompetent to make determinations about proposed treatment plans. They are entitled to a judicial determination as to the propriety of being compelled to take medication over their objection.); Matter of Kornfein, N.Y.L.J., 5/29/98, p. 31, col. 1 (Sup. Ct., Rockland County) (A guardian would not be appointed pursuant to Mental Hygiene Law Article 81 to make decisions concerning the medical care of respondent, an involuntary patient at a state psychiatric center who has been treated with ECT pursuant to prior court orders. Even assuming that respondent was found incapacitated pursuant to Mental Hygiene Law Article 81, to appoint a guardian for the sole purpose of consenting to medical decisions, with unlimited duration, would deprive respondent of her right to make decisions concerning her medical care and would deprive her of due process. Further, since the treatment for which the decision-making power was sought had previously been administered pursuant to court order, the appointment of a Mental Hygiene Law Article 81 guardian would not be necessary.)

§ 22.14 Power to Appoint Guardian—Primary Considerations

PAGE 193:

3. Matter of Maher, cited in Footnote 3, *appeal denied*, 86 N.Y.2d 703, 631 N.Y.S.2d 607, 655 N.E.2d 704 (1995), *reconsideration denied*, 86 N.Y.2d 886, 635 N.Y.S.2d 951, 659 N.E.2d 774 (1995).

5. Matter of Maher, cited in Footnote 5, *appeal denied*, 86 N.Y.2d 703, 631 N.Y.S.2d 607, 655 N.E.2d 704 (1995), *reconsideration denied*, 86 N.Y.2d 886, 635 N.Y.S.2d 951, 659 N.E.2d 774 (1995).

§ 22.15 Power to Appoint Guardian—Jurisdiction

PAGE 194:

[Add to note 6.]

6. See In re Guardianship of Beasley, 234 A.D.2d 32, 650 N.Y.S.2d 170 (1st Dep't, 1996) (although the proposed ward was institutionalized in a facility in Otsego County for more than 20 years, Surrogate's Court, New York County, properly rejected the challenge to its jurisdiction on the ground that there was no showing that the proposed ward ever had the capacity to express an intention to change her domicile from New York County where she was born and where her parents, the petitioners, resided).

§ 22.15

PAGE 195:

[*Add to note 7.*]

7. *See also* Matter of Ackerland, N.Y.L.J., 4/9/96, p. 27, col. 2 (Surr. Ct., N.Y. County) (Jurisdiction of Surrogate's Court under Mental Hygiene Law Article 81 is limited to providing for the property management needs of disabled persons. It benefits a disabled person to have a single court supervise property and personal needs and represents efficient use of resources. If an application for property guardianship is made in Surrogate's Court appears to require a personal needs management, the Surrogate's Court will decline to entertain the application in favor of encouraging a single proceeding in the Supreme Court for guardianship of both person and property. Court directed the guardian *ad litem* to apply to the Supreme Court for the appointment of a Mental Hygiene Law Article 81 guardian for his ward's person and property).

§ 22.16 Power to Appoint Guardian—Venue

PAGE 195:

[*Add to note 1.*]

1. *See* In re Guardianship of Beasley, 234 A.D.2d 32, 650 N.Y.S.2d 170 (1st Dep't, 1996) (although the proposed ward was institutionalized in a facility in Otsego County for more than 20 years, Surrogate's Court, New York County, properly rejected the challenge to its jurisdiction on the ground that there was no showing that the proposed ward ever had the capacity to express an intention to change her domicile from New York County where she was born and where her parents, the petitioners, resided).

[*Add to note 8.*]

8. *See* In re Guardianship of Beasley, 234 A.D.2d 32, 650 N.Y.S.2d 170 (1st Dep't, 1996) (although the proposed ward was institutionalized in a facility in Otsego County Surrogate's Court, New York County, properly refused to transfer venue to Otsego County upon the grounds that petitioners resided in New York County, the court had already expended a great deal of time and effort on the matter, the Law Guardian, who was serving *pro bono*, worked in New York County, and had not been impeded in her tasks by the location of the facility in which her ward was institutionalized, the court could accept responses to written interrogatories from witnesses who were unable to appear in New York County, and applicant Mental Hygiene Legal Service had failed to demonstrate that the convenience of material witnesses or the ends of justice would be served by the transfer).

§ 22.17 Power to Appoint Guardian—Standing to Commence Proceeding

PAGE 196:

[*Add new note 2.1 following "(1) the person alleged to be incapacitate".*]

2.1 *See* Matter of Maier, N.Y.L.J., 2/6/98, p. 28, col. 1 (Sup. Ct., Bronx County) (Alleged incapacitated person brought proceeding for appointment of guardian who would have the power to recoup property from family members which the AIP allegedly transferred as part of a spend down plan. The original application by the AIP was denied because the facts adduced at the hearing did not present clear and convincing evidence that the petitioner had the requisite capacity to consent to the appointment of a guardian. The court authorized conversion of the application to one premised on incapacity. Although the court appointed a guardian, it declined to give the guardian power to recover the transferred property. After independent investigations and reports by the court evaluator and guardian *ad litem*, the court ruled that the potential benefit of such recovery to the AIP was questionable.)

§ 22.20 Proceeding to Appoint Guardian—Time and Method of Service of Notice

PAGE 199:

[*Add to Footnote 5.*]

5. Matter of Barrios–Paoli (Kautsch), 173 Misc.2d 736, 662 N.Y.S.2d 388 (Sup. Ct., Queens County, 1997) (Court granted application to fashion an alternate method of service on the AIP because service by personal delivery could not be effectuated. Court determined that AIP had refused to accept service and allowed petitioner to mail supplemental order to show cause and copy of petition to AIP by regular mail.)

§ 22.27 Court Evaluator—Compensation

PAGE 211:

[*Add to note 1.*]

1. *See also* In re Petty, 256 A.D.2d 281, 682 N.Y.S.2d 183 (1st Dep't, 1998) (Mental Hygiene Law § 81.09(f), providing for an award of a reasonable allowance to a court evaluator, has been applied where a petitioner has stated an intent to withdraw the petition after which the court has dismissed. Similarly, the statute is applicable to circumstances where the petitioners initially sought to withdraw their petition and stipulated to discontinue the proceedings on the court's direction. Further, because the court evaluator's report established that respondent was capable of managing his personal and financial affairs, petitioners' allegations failed to meet the standards for appointment of a guardian. Because of the weakness of the petition, the court evaluator's fee should be borne by the petitioners in its entirety.)

§ 22.28 Court Evaluator—Appointment of Counsel for the Alleged Incompetent Person

PAGE 214:

[*Add to note 18 following Petition of Rocco.*]

18. *But see* In re Elmer "Q", 250 A.D.2d 256, 681 N.Y.S.2d 637 (3d Dep't, 1998) (While the Mental Hygiene Law does not compel the court to assess counsel fees for privately retained counsel, the court in its inherent authority has the discretion to set fees in a Mental Hygiene Law Article 81 proceeding. The utility of court-approved fees for services rendered to an alleged incapacitated person is equally compelling with regard to a privately retained attorney.)

§ 22.31 Hearing and Order—Procedure

PAGE 218:

[*Add to note 10, following "Caveat" paragraph.*]

10. *See* Matter of Maier, N.Y.L.J., 2/6/98, p. 28, col. 1 (Sup. Ct., Bronx County) (example of the extended delays that can occur in a guardianship proceeding, notwithstanding the statutory requirements of speed).

PAGE 219:

[*Add new note 14.1 after "good cause shown" at end of third complete sentence in carryover paragraph.*]

14.1 *See* Application of Barrios–Paoli (Cathy R.), 173 Misc.2d 1032, 662 N.Y.S.2d 925 (Sup. Ct., N.Y. County, 1997) (court granted application to exclude from the courtroom the attorney for AIP's landlord, a non-party, on the ground that such attor-

§ 22.31 GUARDIANSHIP Ch. 22

ney might use the testimony against the AIP in an eviction hearing, except during certain arguments and testimony by witnesses presented by the landlord).

§ 22.32 Hearing and Order—Presence of Person Alleged to be Incapacitated

PAGE 220:

4. Matter of Maher, cited in Footnote 4, *appeal denied*, 86 N.Y.2d 703, 631 N.Y.S.2d 607, 655 N.E.2d 704 (1995), *reconsideration denied*, 86 N.Y.2d 886, 635 N.Y.S.2d 951, 659 N.E.2d 774 (1995).

PAGE 221:

9. Matter of Richman, cited in Footnote 9, is also cited as In re Harriet R., 224 A.D.2d 625, 639 N.Y.S.2d 390 (2d Dep't, 1996), *appeal denied*, 88 N.Y.2d 805, 646 N.Y.S.2d 985, 670 N.E.2d 226 (1996).

12. Matter of Maher, cited in Footnote 12, *appeal denied*, 86 N.Y.2d 703, 631 N.Y.S.2d 607, 655 N.E.2d 704 (1995), *reconsideration denied*, 86 N.Y.2d 886, 635 N.Y.S.2d 951, 659 N.E.2d 774 (1995).

§ 22.33 Hearing and Order—Evidence

PAGE 222:

1. Matter of Maher, cited in Footnote 1, *appeal denied*, 86 N.Y.2d 703, 631 N.Y.S.2d 607, 655 N.E.2d 704 (1995), *reconsideration denied*, 86 N.Y.2d 886, 635 N.Y.S.2d 951, 659 N.E.2d 774 (1995).

PAGE 223:

4. In re Harriet R., cited in Footnote 4, *appeal denied*, 88 N.Y.2d 805, 646 N.Y.S.2d 985, 670 N.E.2d 226 (1996).

[*Add to note 4.*]

4. *Cf.*, Matter of Seidner, N.Y.L.J., 10/8/97, p. 28, col. 4 (Sup. Ct., Nassau County) (Medical evidence was excluded after objection by attorney for AIP, relying on privilege provisions of Civil Practice Law and Rules 4504. The mere fact that a party is forced to defend an action does not permit an inference of waiver by conduct, and the party's simple denial of allegations of such an action does not constitute any affirmative assertion of his condition. While the AIP vehemently opposed the appointment of a guardian for himself, nowhere in his testimony or in his interview by the court evaluator did he discuss or refer to his mental condition, thus there was no waiver of the privilege.)

§ 22.35 Hearing and Order—Findings of the Court—Voluntary Appointment

PAGE 224:

[*Add to note 1.*]

1. *See* Matter of Maier, N.Y.L.J., 2/6/98, p. 28, col. 1 (Sup. Ct., Bronx County) (Alleged incapacitated person brought proceeding for appointment of guardian who would have the power to recoup property from family members which the AIP allegedly transferred as part of a spend down plan. The original application by the AIP was denied because the facts adduced at the hearing did not present clear and convincing evidence that the petitioner had the requisite capacity to consent to the appointment of a guardian. The court authorized conversion of the application to one premised on incapacity. Although the court appointed a guardian, it declined to give the

§ 22.38 Hearing and Order—Dispositional Alternatives

PAGE 227:

4. Matter of Maher, cited in Footnote 4, *appeal denied*, 86 N.Y.2d 703, 631 N.Y.S.2d 607, 655 N.E.2d 704 (1995), *reconsideration denied*, 86 N.Y.2d 886, 635 N.Y.S.2d 951, 659 N.E.2d 774 (1995).

PAGE 228:

[Add new text following note 6:]

Mental Hygiene Law § 81.16(b) does not authorize the involuntary commitment of an incapacitated person by a special guardian. The appointment of a full guardian is required to take such action. Given the loss of liberties involved in the guardianship process and the vulnerability of persons under the guardianship, the court must receive and review basic information about the well being of the ward. In contrast to the situation where a guardian is appointed, the statutory mechanism for the appointment of a special guardian inadequately addresses the liberty concerns of incapacitated persons in the context of an involuntary commitment. The focus of Mental Hygiene Law § 81.16 was intended to be transactional and temporary, and the involuntary commitment to a nursing home, with its severe effect on the individual liberty and autonomy of the ward does not fit this characterization. Discharge of the special guardian after a short duration leaves the incapacitated person without the close protection Mental Hygiene Law Article 81 was intended to provide such persons. The discharge of the special guardian makes the placement of the ward in the nursing effectively irrevocable.[6.1]

6.1 Application of Gambuti (Bowser), 242 A.D.2d 431, 662 N.Y.S.2d 757 (1st Dep't, 1997).

§ 22.39 Hearing and Order—Award of Counsel Fees to Petitioner

PAGE 230:

[Add to note 3.]

3. See Matter of Muro, N.Y.L.J., 4/20/99, p. 30, col. 1 (Sup. Ct., Suffolk County) (At the request of Department of Social Services, nursing home in which AIP was a resident, petitioned for appointment of a special guardian for the purpose of exercising the AIP's right of election in her husband's estate. Following a hearing, the AIP was adjudged incapacitated and a guardian appointed with, however, much broader powers than requested, upon the consent of the parties. The incapacitated person died before issuance of the commission to the guardian and the right of election was not exercised. There were, therefore, only limited funds in the incapacitated person's estate. Counsel for the nursing home sought compensation in excess of $27,000. The court reduced the award of counsel fees, which were payable from the estate of the incapacitated person, to $4,500. While finding that there was no question as to counsel's qualifications in the field of elder law, nor any question of the propriety of the nursing home's commencement of the guardianship proceeding, which

§ 22.39

did result in the appointment of a guardian with the power to exercise the right of election, and approval of the incapacitated person's Medicaid application, significant personal and property management needs were not addressed in the guardianship petition and failure to address such needs is a significant factor to be considered in determining the amount of the legal fee to be awarded the nursing home.)

[*Add new note 4.1 at end of first sentence in second paragraph.*]

4.1 Matter of Grace "PP", 245 A.D.2d 824, 666 N.Y.S.2d 793 (3d Dep't, 1997) (Award of counsel fees to petitioner's attorney, to be paid by respondent, was held proper where there was no evidence in the record of the AIP's indigence, even though there was evidence that the AIP was a Medicaid recipient.)

§ 22.41 Hearing and Order—Person to Be Appointed Guardian—Priority and Criteria for Appointment

PAGE 234:

13. Matter of Lula XX, cited in Footnote 13, *appeal dismissed*, 88 N.Y.2d 842, 644 N.Y.S.2d 683, 667 N.E.2d 333 (1996), *motion dismissed*, 88 N.Y.2d 1040, 651 N.Y.S.2d 13, 673 N.E.2d 1241 (1996).

§ 22.47 Role of Guardian—Powers; Property Management

PAGE 241:

[*Add to note 4 following first paragraph.*]

4. *See* In re Estate of Bernice B., 179 Misc.2d 149, 683 N.Y.S.2d 713 (Surr. Ct., New York County, 1998) (Following jury trial in Surrogate's Court, the court determined that AIP was incapacitated within the meaning of Mental Hygiene Law Article 81 as a result of her "bizarre" behavior during the course of the proceeding to probate the will of her mother and her actions threatened to trigger the *in terrorem* clause in the will which would result in loss of her bequest and her only source of income. The court appointed a guardian for the purpose of accepting any paper required to be served in the administration of the estate or the trust established for the incapacitated person, and to appear in court on her behalf for purposes of any proceeding in Surrogate's Court. However, the court denied the guardian powers to manage the funds the incapacitated person would ultimately receive from the trust since she would not be receiving her interest outright, she appeared able to manage her outlays for daily discretionary costs and the trustee could pay her regular expenses directly.)

§ 22.48 Role of Guardian—Substituted Judgment

PAGE 245:

11. Matter of John "XX", cited in Footnote 11, *appeal denied*, 89 N.Y.2d 814, 659 N.Y.S.2d 854, 681 N.E.2d 1301 (1997).

[*Add at end of note 11.*]

11. *Cf.*, Matter of DiCecco (Gersten), 173 Misc.2d 692, 661 N.Y.S.2d 943 (Sup. Ct., Queens County, 1997) (Court appointed guardian and permitted guardian to transfer AIP's residence and other personal property for the purpose of Medicaid planning. Decision was made upon a finding that it appeared that no period of ineligibility would be imposed as a result of such transfers. The court noted that such transfers did not appear to violate the provisions of § 217 of the Health Insurance Portability and Accountability Act of 1996 which im-

posed criminal penalties for acts involving Medicare and Medicaid.)

The Balanced Budget Act of 1997, effective August 5, 1997, Pub. L. 105–33, included Section 4734, which replaced Section 217 of the Health Insurance Portability and Accountability Act of 1996. Section 217 made it a crime for a person and affiliated parties to make certain transfers of assets in order to obtain Medicaid benefits for nursing home or other long-term care. Section 4734 makes it a crime (misdemeanor) for a paid advisor to knowingly and willingly counsel or assist another to dispose of assets for the purpose of obtaining Medicaid assistance, where the disposition of assets results in the imposition of a Medicaid penalty period.

The impact of this section is that it is the attorney and other paid advisors who may be liable for advising the transfer of assets. However, this section was the subject of a constitutional challenge, as violating the First and Fifth Amendments of the United States Constitution, in *New York State Bar Association v. Reno*, 999 F.Supp. 710 (U.S. Dist. Ct., N.D.N.Y. 1998). Although the Attorney General apparently agreed not to defend the action (Letter from Attorney General to Speaker of the House of Representatives, March 11, 1998), or enforce the law, the District Court issued a preliminary injunction prohibiting enforcement of the law.

§ 22.53 Role of Guardian—Powers; Personal Needs

PAGE 251:

[*Add to note 5 following second paragraph.*]

5. See Matter of New York Presbyterian Hospital (J.H.L.), N.Y.L.J., 6/4/99, p. 33, col. 4 (Sup. Ct., Westchester County) (The finding in a Mental Hygiene Law Article 81 proceeding that a person is incapacitated, does not, as a matter of law, deprive such person of the right to a hearing pursuant to Mental Hygiene Law Article 33 (*Rivers Hearing*) on the issue of whether she should be forcibly medicated. Appointment of a Mental Hygiene Law Article 81 guardian does not deprive a person of the right to refuse a course of treatment, including the forcible administration of psychotropic medications. There is no presumption that such individuals are incompetent to make determinations about proposed treatment plans. They are entitled to a judicial determination as to the propriety of being compelled to take medication over their objection.); Matter of Kornfein, N.Y.L.J., 5/29/98, p. 31, col. 1 (Sup. Ct., Rockland County) (A Mental Hygiene Law Article 81 guardian would not be appointed to make decisions concerning the medical care of respondent, an involuntary patient at a state psychiatric center who has been treated with ECT pursuant to prior court orders. Even assuming that respondent was found incapacitated pursuant to Mental Hygiene Law Article 81, to appoint a guardian for the sole purpose of consenting to medical decisions, with unlimited duration, would deprive respondent of her right to make decisions concerning her medical care and would deprive her of due process. Further, since the treatment for which the decision-making power was sought had previously been administered pursuant to court order, the appointment of a Mental Hygiene Law Article 81 guardian would not be necessary.)

[*Add to note 5 following "Practice Pointer".*]

5. See e.g., Matter of Lowe, N.Y.L.J., 4/16/99, p. 36, col. 6 (Sup. Ct., Queens County) (Consistent with the policy that a guardian should be appointed only as a last resort and should not be imposed if available resources or other alternatives will adequately protect the person, the court refused to appoint a guardian for the sole purpose of appointing a successor health care agent where the primary health care agent was still alive and acting, solely on the ground that the successor agent named by incapacitated person had died. No evidence, much less clear and convincing evidence, had been introduced that the incapacitated person could not name a successor health care agent. Further, the court ruled that under the health care proxy law, only a competent individual may appoint a health care agent who can make health care decisions in the event of the person's incompetence. Selection of a health care agent is a personal decision which can only be made by the competent individual. A court cannot appoint a guardian under Mental Hygiene Law Article 81 with the authority to select an alternative health care agent when a person does not have the capacity to do so for himself.)

§ 22.54 Role of Guardian—Effect of Appointment on Incapacitated Person

PAGE 254:

[Add to note 8.]

8. *See* Matter of Lowe, N.Y.L.J., 4/16/99, p. 36, col. 6 (Sup. Ct., Queens County) (Consistent with the policy that a guardian should be appointed only as a last resort and should not be imposed if available resources or other alternatives will adequately protect the person, the court refused to appoint a guardian for the sole purpose of appointing a successor health care agent where the primary health care agent was still alive and acting, solely on the ground that the successor agent named by incapacitated person had died. No evidence, much less clear and convincing evidence, had been introduced that the incapacitated person could not name a successor health care agent. Further, the court ruled that under the health care proxy law, only a competent individual may appoint a health care agent who can make health care decisions in the event of the person's incompetence. Selection of a health care agent is a personal decision which can only be made by the competent individual. A court cannot appoint a guardian under Mental Hygiene Law Article 81 with the authority to select an alternative health care agent when a person does not have the capacity to do so for himself.)

§ 22.61 Compensation of Guardian

PAGE 260:

[Add to note 5.]

5. *See* Matter of Arnold "O", 256 A.D.2d 764, 681 N.Y.S.2d 627 (3d Dep't, 1998) (The court noted that there were unique circumstances involved in this guardianship. Mental Hygiene Law Article 81 does not provide any definitive formula for fixing guardian compensation. The statutory directive is that the court take into account the specific authority of the guardian to provide for the personal needs and/or property management for the incapacitated person, clearly anticipates that Mental Hygiene Law Article 81 guardianships can involve a mix of both personal care to an incapacitated person and fiscal management of the person's needs. In this case, for the 3½ year period of the application, the incapacitated person was without assets, having only obtained a substantial recovery in litigation, which was to be put in a supplemental needs trust, at the end of this period. Virtually all of the guardianship services related to the incapacitated person's complicated healthcare arrangements, personal visits by the guardian to the incapacitated person, required by psychiatric crises and medical emergencies arising out of his paranoid schizophrenia and paraplegia, and enduring excessive and inappropriate harassing contacts by the incapacitated person's brother and mother, involving almost daily involvement in the guardianship. While Mental Hygiene Law § 81.28(a) allows application of the fee schedule of Surrogate's Court Procedure Act § 2309 to compute guardian compensation, such is appropriate where fiscal management of the incapacitated person's assets constitutes a substantial portion of the guardian's responsibilities. Where, as in the instant case, the litigation settlement did not materialize until the end of the time period for which guardianship compensation was sought and none of the guardian's services related to fiscal management of the asset, it is inappropriate to apply Surrogate's Court Procedure Act § 2309 for the purpose of calculating a single "annual commission" to compensate the guardian for numerous hours of "customary" services he performed over the 3½ year period. The court applied an hourly rate determined to be reasonable ($100/hour) to all the hours petitioner devoted as guardian of the incapacitated person to determine the guardian's reasonable compensation.)

[Add new text following first complete paragraph.]

The court must allow the guardian the necessary and reasonable expenses actually paid.[5.1]

5.1 Estate of Livingston, N.Y.L.J., 6/7/99, p. 33, col. 6 (Sup. Ct., Queens County) (Order appointing guardian provided that guardian's compensation was to be the same as fiduciaries other than trustees as set forth in Surrogate's Court Procedure Act § 2307 as modified by Mental Hygiene Law § 81.28. The Surrogate's Courts, in applying the Surrogate's Court Procedure Act § 2307, have ruled that the routine and incidental expenses that are incurred by a fiduciary, *i.e.*, local travel, meals, postage, telephone, etc., are usually deemed absorbed by the statutory commission. Necessary and reasonable expenses pertains to actual expenditures made by the fiduciary which were necessary to collect, preserve and distribute estate property. In *Livingston*, the court found that there were necessary and reasonable expenses for which the guardian was entitled to reimbursement, *i.e.*, expenditures to preserve the incapacitated person's cooperative apartment, payment of court fees to obtain her commission and the incapacitated person's marriage certificate and for the bond premium. However, the court ruled that the guardian was not entitled to reimburse herself for fax transmissions, photocopies, court service, travel of her clerk to the courthouse to obtain a copy of the order appointing her guardian, and transportation costs for travel to and from the court, to and from the court examiner's office and the nursing home where the incapacitated person resides.)

PAGE 261:

[*Add new text at end of section.*]

Although there are strong protections of the AIP in the Mental Hygiene Law, a problem arises where the AIP is in a nursing home and is indigent. There is no provision in the law for payment of a guardian where the AIP is indigent. Moreover, organizations funded to provide guardians for the indigent may only act in such capacity for persons living in the community and, therefore, may not serve as guardian once an AIP has been admitted to a nursing home. However, notwithstanding admission to a nursing home where the incapacitated person's personal needs are taken care of and the absence of funds to administer, there is still a need to continue a guardianship to visit and report on the condition of the AIP and assure that his or her rights are protected.[8]

8. The court in In re Daisy Pope, N.Y.L.J., 1/12/99, p. 26, col. 2 (Sup. Ct., N.Y. County) noted this dilemma in the Mental Hygiene Law. The problem becomes payment of the guardian fees. The court called for a list of attorneys willing to serve as *pro bono* guardians or amendment of the rules to allow payment of a fee to guardians appointed pursuant to Mental Hygiene Law Article 81 for indigent nursing home patients.

§ 22.69 Removal, Discharge and Resignation of Guardian—Removal

PAGE 271:

[*Add to note 3.*]

3. *See* Matter of Merkert, N.Y.L.J., 11/3/98, p. 30, col. 6 (Sup. Ct., Nassau County) (Court removed guardian because of improper conduct arising from moving the incapacitated person, her father, to a nursing facility out of the state and concealing such move from the court examiner, her brother (incapacitated person's son) and from his family, as well as for violation of the court's restraining order by continuing to access the incapacitated person's funds, failing to timely or properly file her reports with the court examiner, omitting pertinent data and assets from the reports, and generally not being truthful on a number of material facts. Court found that guardian had directed her father's life to the exclusion of other family members and for her own financial benefit. Court ruled she did not act appropriately as guardian.)

§ 22.70 Removal, Discharge and Resignation of Guardian—Discharge or Modification of Powers

PAGE 273:

[*Add new text following note 11.*]

Following the death of the incapacitated person, an issue has arisen concerning the time when a guardian is required to turn over the ward's assets to the personal representative of the estate. The time of the transfer would determine the period in which each fiduciary is accountable and to whom. The Surrogate's Court Procedure Act governs the estate fiduciary and the Mental Hygiene Law governs the guardian. There is, however, no provision in either statute that specifically identifies the point at which a fiduciary whose ward had died must surrender responsibility for the ward's assets to the fiduciary appointed for the deceased ward's estate. The Surrogate's Court Procedure Act provides for the appointment of a personal representative whenever a decedent leaves assets or liabilities. This suggests that the duties of an executor or administrator may not be carried out indirectly through the continued administration of a fiduciary appointed earlier to protect the decedent's interests in her lifetime, who may not necessarily be required to account to the same persons. Further, nothing in Mental Hygiene Law Article 81 provides that the guardian continues to act on behalf of the ward after the ward's death except for the direction that the guardian may pay for the ward's funeral from the ward's assets. Such fiduciary is barred from entering into new transactions after the ward has died. Therefore, absent special circumstances, the authority of a guardian terminates immediately upon the death of the ward and such fiduciary must turn over the ward's assets to the duly appointed personal representative of the ward's estate once such fiduciary has been appointed.[12]

12. *See* Estate of Baron, N.Y.L.J., 5/11/99, p.27, col.5 (Surr. Ct., New York County).

Chapter 23

ELDER LAW

(update prepared in-house)

Table of Sections

Sec.	
23.19	Supplemental Security Income for the Elderly—Financial Eligibility
23.25	Retirement Income from Qualified Plans—Eligibility, Vesting and Accrual
23.26	____ Contribution Limitations
23.32	____ Taxation of Contributions
23.36	Railroad Retirement Benefits
23.39	Benefits for Federal Employees—Civil Service Retirement Act
23.41	Veterans' Benefits
23.43	Medicare—Eligibility and Enrollment
23.46	____ Part A Benefits—Skilled Nursing Facilities
23.48	____ ____ Hospice Care
23.54	____ Administrative and Judicial Appeals—Eligibility for Benefits
23.56	____ ____ Part A Peer Review Organization Decisions
23.60	Supplemental Medical Insurance (Medigap Plans)—Federal and State Regulation of the Industry
23.68	Long Term Care Insurance—Tax Issues
23.74	Medicaid—Resources
23.75	____ Exempt Resources
23.76	____ Transfer of Resources
23.80	____ Spousal Budgeting: Protection of Resources and Income for Community Spouse
23.81	____ Recoveries Against Estates
23.82	____ Liens
23.83	____ Administrative and Judicial Appeals
23.88	Home Care Coverage—Private Insurance
23.90	Hospital Patient Rights—Bill of Rights
23.91	____ Discharge Planning
23.93	Nursing Home Resident Rights—Admission to a Facility
23.94	____ Bill of Rights
23.95	____ Financial Rights
23.97	____ Bed Hold Policy
23.105	Housing Issues—Home Energy Assistance Program ("HEAP")
23.113	Health Care Decision Making—Physician Assisted Suicide
23.115	Tax Issues—Additional Standard Deduction for the Aged and Blind
23.118	____ Medical Deductions

Westlaw Electronic Research

See Westlaw Electronic Research Guide preceding the Summary of Contents.

§ 23.19 Supplemental Security Income for the Elderly—Financial Eligibility

PAGE 349:

[*Note 10 should read as follows.*]

10. 42 U.S.C.A. § 1382(a)(1)(B), 1382(a)(3)(B); 20 C.F.R. § 416.1205.

[*Note 11 should read as follows.*]

11. 42 U.S.C.A. § 1382(a)(2)(B), 1382(a)(3)(A); 20 C.F.R. § 416.1205.

§ 23.25 Retirement Income from Qualified Plans—Eligibility, Vesting and Accrual

PAGE 353:

[*Note that the C.F.R. section cited in note 2 has been reserved.*]

§ 23.26 Retirement Income from Qualified Plans—Contribution Limitations

PAGE 353:

[*Replace note 1 with the following.*]

1. Internal Revenue Code ("I.R.C.") § 401(a)(17).

§ 23.32 Retirement Income from Qualified Plans—Taxation of Contributions

PAGE 355:

[*Replace note 1 with the following.*]

1. I.R.C. § 402(a).

§ 23.36 Railroad Retirement Benefits

PAGE 357:

[*Replace note 2 with the following.*]

2. 45 U.S.C.A. § 231a(c); 20 C.F.R. § 216.60.

[*Note that the C.F.R. section cited in note 7 has been reserved.*]

§ 23.39 Benefits for Federal Employees—Civil Service Retirement Act

PAGE 358:

[*Replace note 2 with the following.*]

2. 5 U.S.C.A. § 8336(a), (b), (f).

Ch. 23 ELDER LAW § 23.43

[*Replace note 4 with the following.*]

4. 5 U.S.C.A. § 8341; 5 C.F.R. § 831.614.

[*In note 5, delete C.F.R. reference.*]

§ 23.41 Veterans' Benefits

PAGE 360:

[*Replace note 12 with the following.*]

12. 38 U.S.C.A. § 1710(b)(2)(A); 38 C.F.R. §§ 17.46, 17.47.

PAGE 361:

[*The three sentences beginning with the last word on page 360 and continuing until the fifth line on page 361 should be deleted, along with corresponding footnotes 13 and 14.*]

[*In note 15, the relevant part of 38 C.F.R. § 17.51 has been re-designated 38 C.F.R. § 17.60. The rest of the citation remains the same, with the Id. referring also to § 17.60.*]

[*Replace note 16 with the following.*]

16. 38 C.F.R. § 3.1600.

[*In the PRACTICE POINTER following note 19, the citation to 38 U.S.C.A. § 7263 should be to 38 U.S.C.A. § 5904(d)(1).*]

§ 23.43 Medicare—Eligibility and Enrollment

PAGE 363:

[*Replace note 6 with the following.*]

6. 42 U.S.C.A. § 426(a); 42 C.F.R. §§ 406.6(b), 406.10(a). However, since enrollment in Part B is voluntary, an individual may decline Part B coverage.

PAGE 364:

[*Replace note 14 with the following.*]

14. 42 U.S.C.A. § 1395q(a)(2)(E); 42 C.F.R. §§ 406.21(c)(3), 407.25(b)(1).

[*Replace note 17 with the following.*]

17. 42 U.S.C.A. § 1395j; 42 C.F.R. §§ 408.4(a)(1) and 408.20(c). In 1997, the Part B Medicare premium was $43.80 per month.

§ 23.46 Medicare—Part A Benefits—Skilled Nursing Facilities

PAGE 365:

[*Replace the citation in note 1 with the following.*]

1. 42 U.S.C.A. § 1395i–3(a).

[*Following the Id. in note 4, replace the citation with the following.*]

4. 42 C.F.R. § 409.33(c).

§ 23.48 Medicare—Part A Benefits—Hospice Care

PAGE 367:

[*Replace the section's first sentence with the following. All footnotes remain unchanged.*]

Terminally ill[1] patients may receive hospice[2] care for two 90 day periods and an unlimited number of subsequent periods of 60 days each during their lifetime.[3]

§ 23.54 Medicare—Administrative and Judicial Appeals—Eligibility for Benefits

PAGE 369:

[*Replace C.F.R. section in note 2 with the following.*]

2. 20 C.F.R. § 404.900(a).

§ 23.56 Medicare—Administrative and Judicial Appeals—Part A Peer Review Organization Decisions

PAGE 371:

[*Replace C.F.R. citation in note 10 with the following.*]

10. 42 C.F.R. § 473.12(b)(2)(i).

[*Replace note 11 with the following.*]

11. 42 C.F.R. § 473.12(b)(2)(ii).

§ 23.60 Supplemental Medical Insurance (Medigap Plans)—Federal and State Regulation of the Industry

PAGE 374:

[*In note 7, replace U.S.C.A. citation with the following.*]

7. 42 U.S.C.A. § 1395ss(q), 1395ss(s).

§ 23.68 Long Term Care Insurance—Tax Issues

PAGE 382:

4. See also Insurance Law § 3229.

PAGE 383:

[*Replace note 7 with the following.*]

7. I.R.C. § 213(d)(1).

§ 23.74 Medicaid—Resources

PAGE 386:

[*Replace note 1 with the following.*]

1. 18 NYCRR § 360–4.4(a).

§ 23.75 Medicaid—Exempt Resources

PAGE 387:

1. *See* 18 NYCRR § 360–4.4(b).

§ 23.76 Medicaid—Transfer of Resources

PAGE 388:

[*In note 2, replace NYCRR citation with the following.*]

2. 18 NYCRR § 360–4.4(c)(1)(iii)(a)(2).

PAGE 389:

[*Replace the first sentence of the page's first full paragraph with the following.*]

The Taxpayer Relief Act of 1997 amended 42 U.S.C.A. § 1320a–7b(a) by providing criminal penalties for whoever "for a fee knowingly and willfully counsels or assists an individual to dispose of assets (including by any transfer in trust) in order for the individual to become eligible for medical assistance under a State plan under subchapter XIX of this chapter, if disposing of the assets results in the imposition of a period of ineligibility for such assistance" under 42 U.S.C.A. § 1396p(c).

[*Delete note 4.*]

PAGE 391:

[*In note 20, correct citation to Matter of Driscoll.*]

20. Matter of Driscoll, N.Y.L.J., 10/22/93, p.30, col.4 (Sup.Ct., Nassau County).

§ 23.80 Medicaid—Spousal Budgeting: Protection of Resources and Income for Community Spouse

PAGE 396:

[*The sentence beginning eight lines from the bottom of the page ("The spouse has the right . . . institutionalized spouse's income.") should be re-written to read as follows.*]

The spouse has the right to insist on an enhanced CSRA to generate the MMMNA, and the income may be provided from either the income or resources of the institutionalized spouse.

[*The change in the text is a result of the decision in Golf v. Department of Social Services being reversed by the Court of Appeals. Consequently, the citation in note 13 should be to the Court of Appeals decision.*]

13. Golf v. New York State Department of Social Services, 91 N.Y.2d 656, 662, 674 N.Y.S.2d 600, 603, 697 N.E.2d 555, 558 (1998).

PAGE 397:

[*In note 21, replace the NYCRR citation with the following.*]

21. 18 NYCRR § 360–4.10(c)(1)(iii).

§ 23.81 Medicaid—Recoveries Against Estates

PAGE 399:

[*In note 13, change spelling of "Brickel" to "Brickell".*]

§ 23.82 Medicaid—Liens

PAGE 399:

[*In note 2, the correct citation for the case cited is:*]

2. Cricchio v. Pennisi, 90 N.Y.2d 296, 660 N.Y.S.2d 679, 683 N.E.2d 301 (1997), on remand to Link v. Town of Smithtown, 175 Misc.2d 238, 670 N.Y.S.2d 692 (1997).

PAGE 400:

[*Replace note 5 with the following.*]

5. 18 NYCRR §§ 360–7.2, 360–7.11(b)(5).

§ 23.83 Medicaid—Administrative and Judicial Appeals

PAGE 400:

[*Replace note 3 with the following.*]

3. 18 NYCRR §§ 358–3.5, 360–2.9.

§ 23.88 Home Care Coverage—Private Insurance
PAGE 406:

[*Replace note 2 with the following.*]

  2. 11 NYCRR § 52.22(d)(6)(x).

[*In note 4, replace the citation with the following.*]

  4. 11 NYCRR § 52.22(d)(6)(x)(4).

§ 23.90 Hospital Patient Rights—Bill of Rights
PAGE 407:

[*Replace note 9 with the following.*]

  9. 10 NYCRR § 405.7(b)(4).

[*Replace note 10 with the following.*]

  10. 10 NYCRR § 405.7(b)(6).

§ 23.91 Hospital Patient Rights—Discharge Planning
PAGE 410:

[*Replace note 22 with the following.*]

  22. 18 NYCRR § 505.20(b)(3)(ii).

[*Replace both citations in note 23 with the following.*]

  23. 18 NYCRR § 505.20(b)(3)(iii).

§ 23.93 Nursing Home Resident Rights—Admission to a Facility
PAGE 412:

[*In note 2, replace the NYCRR citation with the following.*]

  2. 10 NYCRR § 405.9(f).

PAGE 413:

[*In note 14, replace C.F.R. citation with the following.*]

  14. 42 C.F.R. § 483.102(b)(1).

§ 23.94 Nursing Home Resident Rights—Bill of Rights
PAGE 414:

[*Replace note 7 with the following.*]

  7. 10 NYCRR § 415(c)(2)(ii)(b).

§ 23.95 Nursing Home Resident Rights—Financial Rights

PAGE 415:

[*Replace Public Health Law citation with the following.*]

Public Health Law § 2803–c(3)(d).

PAGE 416:

3. Note that since 1994, 42 U.S.C.A. § 1395–3(c)(6)(B) has required the facility to deposit personal funds in excess of $100 (rather than $50) in an interest bearing account, and has allowed funds less than $100 to be kept in a non-interest bearing account or petty cash fund. The C.F.R. and NYCRR keep the $50 amount.

[*In note 5, replace the C.F.R. citation with the following.*]

5. 42 C.F.R. § 483.10(b)(5).

§ 23.97 Nursing Home Resident Rights—Bed Hold Policy

PAGE 417:

[*In note 1, citation to 42 U.S.C.A. § 1395i–3(c)(2)(D) should be deleted.*]

PAGE 418:

[*Replace note 4 with the following.*]

4. 18 NYCRR § 505.9(d)(6)(iii)(a).

[*Replace note 5 with the following.*]

5. 18 NYCRR § 505.9(d)(6)(i).

§ 23.105 Housing Issues—Home Energy Assistance Program ("HEAP")

PAGE 424:

[*Replace note 3 with the following.*]

3. 18 NYCRR § 393.4(c)(3).

§ 23.113 Health Care Decision Making—Physician Assisted Suicide

PAGE 431:

[*Replace last citation in note 1 with the following.*]

1. Penal Law § 125.15(1).

PAGE 432:

[*Replace note 2 with the following.*]

2. 521 U.S. 793, 117 S.Ct. 2293, 138 L.Ed.2d 834 (1997).

[*Replace note 3 with the following.*]

3. 521 U.S. 702, 117 S.Ct. 2258, 138 L.Ed.2d 772 (1997).

§ 23.115 Tax Issues—Additional Standard Deduction for the Aged and Blind

PAGE 433:

[*The first sentence of the first full paragraph on the page should read as follows.*]

If an elderly or blind taxpayer is claimed as a dependent on another's return, the basic standard deduction for the elderly or disabled person is the greater of $500, or the sum of $250 and such individual's earned income.[6]

§ 23.118 Tax Issues—Medical Deductions

PAGE 434:

[*Replace note 7 with the following.*]

7. I.R.C. § 7702B.

Chapter 24

ESTATE PLANNING

by
Gideon Rothschild*

Table of Sections

24.10	Wills—Provisions—Debts and Taxes
24.12	___ Provisions—Residuary Estate
24.16	___ ___ Fiduciary Powers
24.17	___ ___ Miscellaneous
24.20	New York State Estate and Gift Tax
24.28	Generation Skipping Transfer Tax—Generation Assignment
24.32	Charitable Bequests
24.34	Planning With Certain Assets—Life Insurance
24.35	___ ___ Life Insurance Trusts
24.38	___ Closely Held Business Interests
24.40	___ ___ Liquidity Issues
24.41	___ ___ Minority Discounts
24.45	Lifetime Planning—Valuation of Gifts
24.47	___ Valuation of Gifts—Residence Trusts
24.48	___ Valuation of Gifts—Residence Trusts—Income Tax Considerations
24.51	___ Annual Gift Tax Exclusion—Uniform Transfers to Minor's Act Accounts
24.53	___ Annual Gift Tax Exclusion
24.54	___ Charitable Remainder Trusts
24.68	Postmortem Planning—Disclaimers
24.73	___ Electing Alternate Valuation Date
24.74	___ Allocation of Income and Expenses
24.82	Probate Avoidance—Totten Trusts
24.83	___ Jointly Held Assets
24.84	Asset Protection
24.85	___ Statutory Exemptions

* **NOTE: GIDEON ROTHSCHILD** is now a partner with the New York City law firm of MOSES & SINGER LLP, concentrating in estate planning and asset protection planning. He is a member of the Advisory Boards of BNA Tax Management, American Academy of Estate Planning Attorneys, the Journal of Asset Protection, The Practical Accountant, Offshore Finance USA and Keeping Current. He is the co-author of the forthcoming revised portfolio on Asset Protection Planning published by BNA Tax Management and has authored numerous articles for publications including the New York Law Journal, Journal of Asset Protection and Estate Planning.

Mr. Rothschild is the Chair of the Committee on Asset Protection of the American Bar Association and a member of the Offshore Institute, the Estate Planning Council of New York and the Association of the Bar of the City of New York. He has lectured frequently on asset protection and estate planning to professional groups including the New York University Federal Tax Institute, the New York State Bar Association, the American Bar Association and the American Institute of Certified Public Accountants. Mr. Rothschild holds a B.B.A. from Baruch College (1973) and J.D. from New York Law School and is also licensed as a Certified Public Accountant.

24.95 Ethical Considerations in Estate Planning—Attorney/Draftsman as Fiduciary or Beneficiary

Westlaw Electronic Research

See Westlaw Electronic Research Guide preceding the Summary of Contents.

---

§ 24.10 Wills—Provisions—Debts and Taxes

PAGE 457:

[*Replace EPTL citation in note 3 with the following.*]

3. EPTL § 1–2.17.

§ 24.12 Wills—Provisions—Residuary Estate

PAGE 459:

[*Replace note 2 with the following.*]

2. See EPTL § 3–3.7(a) which permits dispositions to intervivos trusts executed in the manner provided for in EPTL § 7–1.17.

§ 24.16 Wills—Provisions—Fiduciary Powers

PAGE 462:

[*In item "(6)" at end of section, delete the word "and" and replace the semi-colon at the end of sentence with a period.*]

§ 24.17 Wills—Provisions—Miscellaneous

PAGE 462:

[*Replace note 1 with the following.*]

1. EPTL § 7–6.5.

[*In last sentence of paragraph entitled, "Minors Provision", substitute "$10,000" for "$5,000".*]

[*In note 2, replace EPTL citation with the following.*]

2. EPTL § 11–1.1(b)(19).

§ 24.20 New York State Estate and Gift Tax

PAGE 468:

[*Replace note 5 with the following.*]

5. Tax Law § 955(f).

§ 24.28 Generation Skipping Transfer Tax—Generation Assignment

PAGE 475:

[*Replace note 3 with the following.*]

3. I.R.C. § 2651(e).

§ 24.32 Charitable Bequests

PAGE 479:

[*Replace note 6 with the following.*]

6. I.R.C. § 2522.

§ 24.34 Planning With Certain Assets—Life Insurance

PAGE 479:

[*Replace note 2 with the following.*]

2. I.R.C. § 2035(a)(2).

[*Add following note 5.*]

5. **PRACTICE POINTER:** To avoid a taxable gift if the value exceeds the available annual exclusion consider borrowing out some of the cash value.

CAVEAT: The transfer of a policy for consideration (which exists when there is a loan on the policy) may trigger the transfer for value rule. This result can be avoided by transferring the policy to either the insured, or partner of the insured, a partnership in which the insured is a partner or a corporation in which the insured is a shareholder or officer, or if the basis in the hands of the donee is determined by reference to the basis of the donor. I.R.C. § 101(a)(2).

§ 24.35 Planning With Certain Assets—Life Insurance—Life Insurance Trusts

PAGE 480:

[*Replace note 2 with the following.*]

2. I.R.C. § 2035(a)(2).

§ 24.38 Planning With Certain Assets—Closely Held Business Interests

PAGE 484:

[*Replace note 1 with the following.*]

1. The Qualified Family-Owned Business Interest Exclusion enacted by the Taxpayer Relief Act of 1997 and codified at I.R.C. § 2033A, was converted into a deduction and redesignated as I.R.C. § 2057 by the Internal Revenue Service Restructuring and Reform Act of 1998 (P.L. 105–206), in part, to clarify the interaction of that section with other estate tax provisions. Unlike the exclusion (which was set to decrease in lock-step with the phase-in of the unified credit to $1,000,000 by the year 2006), the deduction is capped at $675,000 and coordinated with the unified credit so that if the qualified family-owned business interest deduction is elected, the applicable exclusion amount will be $625,000 regardless of the year of the decedent's death,

subject to increase, however, on a dollar-for-dollar basis, to the extent that the estate is unable to elect the full $675,000 qualified family-owned business interest deduction so that the combined deduction is equal to $1.3 million. However, the unified credit amount cannot exceed the amount allowed under Code Section 2010.

CAVEAT: Since the family owned business deduction is subject to recapture if the heirs fail to qualify within 10 years after the decedent's death, it will be more advantageous to utilize the unified credit over the family owned business deduction where possible. Example: Business owner dies in 1999 with an estate of $600,000 which includes a business interest worth $400,000. The estate should utilize the unified credit rather than the Sec. 2057 deduction.

§ 24.40 Planning With Certain Assets—Closely Held Business Interests—Liquidity Issues

PAGE 487:

[*Replace note 4 with the following.*]

4. For estates of decedents dying before January 1, 1998 the interest rate was 4% on the lesser of (1) $345,800 less the allowable unified credit, or (2) the amount of estate tax extended under this election. The interest paid was deductible as an administration expense.

[*In note 9, replace I.R.C. citation with the following.*]

9. I.R.C. § 2034(a)(2).

§ 24.41 Planning With Certain Assets—Closely Held Business Interests—Minority Discounts

PAGE 488:

[*Add to end of note 2.*]

2. *Estate of Desmond v. Commissioner*, T.C. Memo. 1999–76, 77 T.C.M. (CCH) 1529 (U.S. Tax Ct. 1999); *Estate of Simplot v. Commissioner*, 112 T.C.No. 13 (U.S. Tax Ct. 1999).

[*Add to end of Practice Pointer.*]

The 3 year statute of limitations on gift tax valuations applies only where the taxpayer adequately discloses on the return the nature of the gift and basis for value reported. Prop. Reg. § 301.6501(c)–1(f).

§ 24.45 Lifetime Planning—Valuation of Gifts

PAGE 490:

[*Add to end of second CAVEAT in note 3.*]

3. See also Private Letter Ruling 9842003. But cf. *Estate of Nowell v. Commissioner*, T.C. Memo. 1999–15, T.C.M. (RIA) 99015 (U.S. Tax Ct. 1999).

§ 24.47 Lifetime Planning—Valuation of Gifts—Residence Trusts

PAGE 492:

[*Replace note 3 with the following.*]

3. Treas. Reg. § 25.2702–5(c)(3).

§ 24.48 Lifetime Planning—Valuation of Gifts—Residence Trusts—Income Tax Considerations

PAGE 493:

[*In third sentence of first paragraph, add the word "principal" immediately prior to the word "residence".*]

PAGE 494:

[*In middle paragraph, substitute Treas. Reg. § 25.2702-5(b)(1) and (c)(9) for Prop. Treas. Reg. § 25.2702-5(b)(1) and (c)(9).*]

§ 24.51 Lifetime Planning—Annual Gift Tax Exclusion—Uniform Transfers to Minor's Act Accounts

PAGE 496:

[*In note 2, replace first EPTL citation with the following.*]

2. EPTL § 7-6.21.

§ 24.53 Lifetime Planning—Annual Gift Tax Exclusion

PAGE 497:

2. But cf. *See* Private Letter Ruling 9751003.

[*In note 3, add to end of first sentence.*]

3. and annual exclusion.

§ 24.54 Lifetime Planning—Charitable Remainder Trusts

PAGE 498:

[*Replace note 6 with the following.*]

6. I.R.C. § 642(c)(3).

§ 24.68 Postmortem Planning—Disclaimers

PAGE 510:

[*In note 4, substitute Treasury Regulation § 25.2518–2 for Proposed Treasury Regulation § 25.2518–2.*]

§ 24.73 Postmortem Planning—Electing Alternate Valuation Date

PAGE 514:

[*Replace EXAMPLE in text with the following.*]

EXAMPLE: Wanda Widow dies on January 1st, 1998 owning only one asset: 100,000 shares of Gizmos, Inc. common stock. Wanda purchased her 100,000 shares at $5 per share. The per share value of Wanda's Gizmos, Inc. stock is $9 per share on the date of her death. Suppose that the per share value decreases to $6 per share on July 1st, the six month anniversary of Wanda's death, but most experts expect that the shares will trade at $9 per share in another year when Wanda's sole beneficiary is planning on selling the stock. Wanda's beneficiary is in the highest tax bracket for income tax purposes, so his capital gains will be taxed at 20%.

In this case, the executor should elect to value the estate as of the alternate valuation date. If the estate were valued as of the date of death, it would be valued at $900,000 (100,000 shares at $9 per share), which, after the unified credit were applied, would incur a federal estate tax of $104,750. Wanda's beneficiary would obtain a tax basis in the stock of $9 per share, and upon sale at $9 per share, would have no capital gains. Thus, date of death valuation would lead to a total tax of $104,750. If alternate valuation date is used, there will be no federal estate tax (due to the unified credit), and the beneficiary will obtain a basis of $6 per share. Upon a later sale at $9 per share, the beneficiary would recognize a $300,000 capital gain ($900,000 amount realized less tax basis of $600,000) and incur a capital gains tax of $60,000. Thus, using the alternate valuation would lead to a total tax of $60,000, for a savings of $44,750 to the beneficiary.

§ 24.74 Postmortem Planning—Allocation of Income and Expenses

PAGE 515:

[*Replace second-to-last sentence of second paragraph with the following.*]

The maximum income tax rate on an estate is 39.6%, which applies to estates with taxable income exceeding $8,350 in 1999.

§ 24.82 Probate Avoidance—Totten Trusts

PAGE 519:

[*In note 1, insert the words "case of" immediately prior to "In re Totten, 179 N.Y. 112, 71 N.E. 748 (1904)."*]

§ 24.83 Probate Avoidance—Jointly Held Assets

PAGE 520:

[*In note 3, substitute Treas. Reg. § 25.2511-1(h)(4) for Treas. Reg. § 25.2511-1(h)(1).*]

§ 24.84 Asset Protection

PAGE 521:

[*Delete note 1.*]

§ 24.85 Asset Protection—Statutory Exemptions

PAGE 521:

[*Add to end of first paragraph.*]

Life insurance proceeds and avails and annuities are also exempt from creditors under New York law.[2.1]

2.1 New York Insurance Law § 3212.

§ 24.95 Ethical Considerations in Estate Planning—Attorney/Draftsman as Fiduciary or Beneficiary

PAGE 528:

[*At the beginning of the fourth sentence of the first paragraph, substitute SCPA § 2307-a for SCPA § 2307A.*]

[*In note 3, replace SCPA citation with the following.*]

3. SCPA § 2307-a.

Chapter 25

PROBATE AND ESTATE ADMINISTRATION

(Update prepared in-house)

Table of Sections

25.46 Compensation of Executor and Administrator, When Payable
25.47 Attorney's Fees
25.52 Form—Probate Petition
25.53 ____ Affidavit Proving Correct Copy of Will
25.54 ____ Citation in Probate
25.55 ____ Affidavit of Service of Citation
25.57 ____ Waiver and Consent
25.58 ____ Notice of Probate
25.59 ____ Deposition Affidavit of Subscribing Witness
25.61 ____ Decree Granting Probate

Westlaw Electronic Research

See Westlaw Electronic Research Guide preceding the Summary of Contents.

§ 25.46 Compensation of Executor and Administrator, When Payable

PAGE 592:

[Append to this section the following.]

SCPA § 2307-a specifically governs attorneys as executors and imposes additional duties upon lawyers who choose to act as executors. It requires attorneys to disclose to the testator a) that anyone can serve as an executor, not just an attorney; b) that any executor is entitled to the statutory commission, absent a contrary agreement; and c) that if an attorney or an affiliated attorney performs legal services in connection with the executor's official duties, that attorney is entitled to receive just and reasonable compensation for such legal services, in addition to the executor's statutory commissions.[11] § 2307-a further requires that the testator acknowledge the disclosure in writing.[12] If § 2307-a is not complied with, then the attorney-executor would only be entitled to ½ of the normal statutory entitlement.[13] In such a case, the additional commissions set forth under § 2307(6) are not affected, although those set forth under the remainder of § 2307 and § 2313 are halved.[14]

11. SCPA § 2307-a(1).

12. SCPA § 2307-a(2).

§ 25.46 PROBATE AND ESTATE ADMINISTRATION Ch. 25

13. SCPA § 2307–a(5).
14. SCPA § 2307–a(6).

§ 25.47 Attorney's Fees

PAGE 592:

[*Replace note 2 with the following.*]

2. Matter of Estate of Wiggins, 200 A.D.2d 813, 606 N.Y.S.2d 423 (3d Dep't. 1994), *affirmed as modified by* Stortecky v. Mazzone, 85 N.Y.2d 518, 626 N.Y.S.2d 733, 650 N.E.2d 391 (1995). *See also*, Turano, 1991 Supp. Practice Commentary to SCPA 2307.

[*Replace note 3 with the following.*]

3. Wiggins, supra note 2.

PAGE 593:

[*Append to the end of this section.*]

SCPA § 2307–a has been recently added to the SCPA, and it contains important provisions related to attorneys who act as executors. The section requires attorneys to disclose to the testator a) that anyone can serve as an executor, not just an attorney; b) that any executor is entitled to the statutory commission, absent a contrary agreement; and c) that if an attorney or an affiliated attorney performs legal services in connection with the executor's official duties, that attorney is entitled to receive just and reasonable compensation for such legal services, in addition to the executor's statutory commissions.[10] § 2307–a further requires that the testator acknowledge the disclosure in writing.[11] If § 2307–a is not complied with, then the attorney-executor would only be entitled to ½ of the normal statutory entitlement.[12] In such a case, the additional commissions authorized under § 2307(6) are not affected, although those set forth under the remainder of § 2307 and § 2313 are halved.[13]

10. SCPA § 2307–a(1).
11. SCPA § 2307–a(2).
12. SCPA § 2307–a(5).
13. SCPA § 2307–a(6).

Ch. 25 PROBATE AND ESTATE ADMINISTRATION § 25.52

§ 25.52 Form—Probate Petition

Form P-1 (1/99)

SURROGATE'S COURT OF THE STATE OF NEW YORK
COUNTY OF

Probate Proceeding, Will of

_____
Deceased.

PETITION FOR PROBATE AND:
☐ Letters Testamentary
☐ Letters of Trusteeship
☐ Letters of Administration c.t.a.

File No. _____ –19 _____

TO THE SURROGATE'S COURT, County of :

It is respectfully alleged:

1. (a) The name, citizenship, domicile (or, in the case of a bank or trust company, its principal office) and interest in this proceeding of the petitioner are as follows:

Name _____ Citizenship ☐ U.S.A.
Domicile or principal office: _____ (check one) ☐ Other _____
                                                                                                  specify

_____
                          Street and Number

_____
        City, Village or Town   State   Zip Code
Mailing address (if different from domicile) _____

Name _____ Citizenship ☐ U.S.A.
Domicile or principal office: _____ (check one) ☐ Other _____
                                                                                                  specify

_____
                          Street and Number

_____
        City, Village or Town   State   Zip Code
Mailing address (if different from domicile) _____

Interest(s) of Petitioner(s):   ☐ Executor(s) named in decedent's Will
(check one)   ☐ Other (specify) _____

(b) The proposed Executor ☐ is ☐ is not an attorney.
▶[NOTE: An Executor-Attorney must comply with SCPA 2307-a.]

2. The name, domicile, date and place of death, and national citizenship of the above-named decedent are as follows:
   (a) Name _____
   (b) Date of death _____
   (c) Place of death _____
   (d) Domicile _____
                                                Street Address

   _____
     City/Town/Village   County   State
   (e) Citizenship ☐ U.S.A.
       (check one) ☐ Other (specify) _____

3. The Last Will, herewith presented, relates to both real and personal property and consists of an instrument or instruments dated as shown below and signed at the end thereof by the decedent and the following attesting witnesses:

Date of Will	Names of all Witnesses to Will
Date of Codicil	Names of all Witnesses to Codicil
Date of Codicil	Names of all Witnesses to Codicil

4. No other will or codicil of the decedent is on file in this Surrogate's Court, and upon information and belief, after a diligent search and inquiry, including a search of any safe deposit box, there exists no will, codicil or other testamentary instrument of the decedent later in date to any of the instruments mentioned in paragraph 3 except as follows: [Enter "NONE" or specify][1]

§ 25.52   PROBATE AND ESTATE ADMINISTRATION   Ch. 25

5. The decedent was survived by distributees classified as follows:
▶ [Information is required only as to those classes of surviving relatives who would take the property of decedent pursuant to EPTL 4-1.1 and 4-1.2. State number of survivors in each class. Insert "NO" in all prior classes. Insert "X" in all subsequent classes.]

    a. [   ] Spouse (husband/wife).
    b. [   ] Child or children and/or issue of predeceased child or children. [Must include marital, nonmarital, adopted, or adopted-out child under DRL Section 117]
    c. [   ] Mother/Father.
    d. [   ] Sisters and/or brothers, either of the whole or half blood, and issue of predeceased sisters and/or brothers (nieces/nephews, etc.).
    e. [   ] Grandparents. [Include maternal and paternal]
    f. [   ] Aunts and/or uncles, and children of predeceased aunts and/or uncles (first cousins). [Include maternal and paternal]
    g. [   ] First cousins once removed (children of predeceased first cousins). [Include maternal and paternal]

6. The names, relationships, domicile and addresses of all distributees (under EPTL 4-1.1 and 4-1.2), of each person designated in the Will herewith presented as primary executor, of all persons adversely affected by the purported exercise by such Will of any power of appointment, of all persons adversely affected by any codicil and of all persons having an interest under any other will of the decedent on file in the Surrogate's Court, are hereinafter set forth in subdivisions (a) and (b).
▶ [If the propounded will purports to revoke or modify an inter vivos trust or any other testamentary substitute, list the names, relationships, domicile and addresses of the trustee and beneficiaries affected by the will in subparagraphs (a) and (b) below. Submit trust agreement.]

(a) All persons and parties so interested who are of full age and sound mind or which are corporations or associations, are as follows:

Name and Relationship	Domicile Address and Mailing Address	Description of Legacy, Devise or Other Interest, or Nature of Fiduciary Status, in the Will

(b) All persons so interested who are persons under disability, are as follows: ▶ [Furnish all information specified in NOTE following 7b]

Name and Relationship	Domicile Address and Mailing Address	Description of Legacy, Devise or Other Interest, or Nature of Fiduciary Status, in the Will

7. The names and domiciliary addresses of all substitute or successor executors and of all trustees, guardians, legatees, devisees, and other beneficiaries named in the Will and/or trustees and beneficiaries of any inter vivos trust designated in the propounded Will, other than those named in paragraph 6 herewith, are hereinafter set forth in subdivisions (a) and (b).

(a) All such fiduciaries, legatees, devisees, and other beneficiaries who are of full age and sound mind or which are corporations or associations, are as follows:

Name	Domicile Address and Mailing Address	Description of Legacy, Devise or Other Interest, or Nature of Fiduciary Status, in the Will

Ch. 25 PROBATE AND ESTATE ADMINISTRATION § 25.52

(b) All such persons interested who are persons under disability are as follows: ▶[Furnish all information specified in NOTE below]

| Name | Domicile Address and Mailing Address | Description of Legacy, Devise or Other Interest, or Nature of Fiduciary Status, in the Will |

▶[NOTE: In the case of each infant, state (a) name, birth date, relationship to decedent, domicile and residence address, and the person with whom he/she resides, (b) whether or not he/she has a court-appointed guardian (if not, so state), and whether or not his/her father and/or mother is living, and (c) the name and residence address of any court-appointed guardian and the information regarding such appointment. In the case of each other person under a disability, state (a) name, relationship to decedent, and residence address, (b) facts regarding his/her disability including whether or not a committee, conservator, guardian, or any other fiduciary has been appointed and whether or not he/she has been committed to any institution, and (c) the names and addresses of any committee, person or institution having care and custody of him/her, conservator, guardian, and any relative or friend having an interest in his/her welfare. In the case of a person confined as a prisoner, state place of incarceration and list any person having an interest in his/her welfare. In the case of unknowns, describe such person in the same language as will be used in the process.]

8. (a) No beneficiary under the propounded will, listed in Paragraph 6 or 7 above, had a confidential relationship to the decedent, such as attorney, accountant, doctor, or clergyperson, except: [Enter "NONE" or indicate the nature of the confidential relationship] _____

(b) No persons, corporations or associations are interested in this proceeding other than those mentioned above.

9. (a) To the best of the knowledge of the undersigned, the approximate total value of all property constituting the decedent's gross testamentary estate is greater than $_____ but less than $_____.
Personal property $_____ Improved real property in New York State $_____
Unimproved real property in New York State $_____
Estimated gross rents for a period of 18 months $_____

(b) No other testamentary assets exist in New York State, nor does any cause of action exist on behalf of the estate, except as follows: [Enter "NONE" or specify] _____

10. Upon information and belief, no other petition for the probate of any will of the decedent or for letters of administration of the decedent's estate has heretofore been filed in any court.

WHEREFORE, your petitioner(s) pray(s): (a) that process be issued to all necessary parties to show cause why the Will and the Codicil(s) set forth in paragraph 3 and presented herewith should not be admitted to probate; (b) that an order be granted directing the service of process, pursuant to the provisions of Article 3 of the SCPA, upon the persons named in paragraph 6 hereof whose names and whereabouts are unknown and cannot be ascertained, or who may be persons on whom service by personal delivery cannot be made; and (c) that such Will and Codicil(s) be admitted to probate as a Will of real and personal property and that letters issue thereon as follows: [Check and complete all relief requested]

☐ Letters Testamentary to _____
☐ Letters of Trusteeship to _____ f/b/o _____
_____ f/b/o _____
☐ Letters of Administration c.t.a. to _____

and that petitioner(s) have such other relief as may be proper.

Dated: _____

1. _____   3. _____
   Signature of Petitioner   Name of Corporate Petitioner
   _____
   Print Name

2. _____   _____
   Signature of Petitioner   Signature of Officer
   _____   _____
   Print Name   Print Name and Title of Officer

COMBINED VERIFICATION, OATH AND DESIGNATION
[For use when petitioner is an individual]

STATE OF
COUNTY OF } ss.:

The undersigned, the petitioner named in the foregoing petition, being duly sworn, says:

1. **VERIFICATION:** I have read the foregoing petition subscribed by me and know the contents thereof, and the same is true of my own knowledge, except as to the matters therein stated to be alleged upon information and belief, and as to those matters I believe it to be true.

2. **OATH OF**
   ☐ EXECUTOR
   ☐ ADMINISTRATOR c.t.a.
   ☐ TRUSTEE

   as indicated above: I am over eighteen (18) years of age and a citizen of the United States and I will well, faithfully and honestly discharge the duties of Fiduciary of the goods, chattels and credits of said decedent according to law. I am not ineligible to receive letters and will duly account for all moneys and other property that will come into my hands.

3. **DESIGNATION OF CLERK FOR SERVICE OF PROCESS:** I hereby designate the Clerk of the Surrogate's Court of Kings County, and his/her successor in office, as a person on whom service of any process issuing from such Court may be made in like manner and with like effect as if it were served personally upon me, whenever I cannot be found and served within the State of New York after due diligence used.

My domicile is _____
                    Street Address

_____
City/Town/Village   State   Zip

_____
           Signature of Petitioner

_____
                Print Name

On _____, 19_____
before me personally came
to me known to be the person described in and who executed the foregoing instrument. Such person duly swore to such instrument before me and duly acknowledged that he/she executed the same.

_____
              Notary Public
       (Affix Notary Stamp or Seal)

COMBINED CORPORATE VERIFICATION, CONSENT AND DESIGNATION
[For use when a petitioner to be appointed is a bank or trust company]

STATE OF
COUNTY OF } ss.:

I, the undersigned, a _____ of
                          Title
_____,
Name of Bank or Trust Company
a corporation duly qualified to act in a fiduciary capacity without further security, being duly sworn, say:

1. **VERIFICATION:** I have read the foregoing petition subscribed by me and know the contents thereof, and the same is true of my own knowledge, except as to the matters therein stated to be alleged upon information and belief, and as to those matters I believe it to be true.

2. **CONSENT:** I consent to accept the appointment as
   ☐ EXECUTOR
   ☐ ADMINISTRATOR c.t.a.
   ☐ TRUSTEE
   under the Last Will and Testament of the decedent described in the foregoing petition and consent to act as such fiduciary.

3. **DESIGNATION OF CLERK FOR SERVICE OF PROCESS:** I designate the Chief Clerk of the Surrogate's Court of Kings County, and his/her successor in office, as a person on whom service of any process issuing from such Surrogate's Court may be made, in like manner and whenever one of its proper officers cannot be found and served within the State of New York after due diligence used.

_____
       Name of Bank or Trust Company

By _____
              Signature

_____
          Print Name and Title

On _____, 19_____
before me personally came
to me known, who duly swore to the foregoing instrument and who did say that he/she resides at _____
and that he/she is a _____
of _____
the corporation / national banking association described in and which executed such instrument, and that he/she signed his/her name thereto by order of the Board of Directors of the corporation / national banking association.

_____
              Notary Public
       (Affix Notary Stamp or Seal)

Signature of Attorney _____   Print Name _____
Firm Name _____   Tel. No. _____
Address of Attorney _____

Ch. 25 PROBATE AND ESTATE ADMINISTRATION § 25.53

§ 25.53 Forms—Affidavit Proving Correct Copy of Will

Form P-13 (12/96)

[Note: Attach a copy of the Will/Codicil to this Affidavit of Comparison executed by any two persons; if a photocopy of the Will is used, only one person need make the affidavit.]

SURROGATE'S COURT OF THE STATE OF NEW YORK
COUNTY OF

Probate Proceeding, Will of

_____

Deceased.

AFFIDAVIT OF COMPARISON

File No. _____ –19_____

STATE OF
COUNTY OF } ss.:

I/We, _____
[and _____], being duly sworn, say(s), that [he/she has] [we have] carefully compared the copy of decedent's Will/Codicil propounded herein to which this affidavit is annexed with the original Will dated the _____ day of _____, 19_____ [and the original Codicil(s) dated the _____ day of _____, 19_____, and the _____ day of _____, 19_____], about to be filed for probate, and that the same is in all respects a true and correct copy of said original Will/Codicil and of the whole thereof.

_____
Signature

_____
Print Name

_____
Signature

_____
Print Name

Sworn to before me this _____ day of
_____, 19_____

_____
Notary Public
(Affix Notary Stamp or Seal)

§ 25.54 PROBATE AND ESTATE ADMINISTRATION Ch. 25

§ 25.54 Forms—Citation in Probate

Form P-5 (7/99)

PROBATE CITATION　　　　　　　　　　　　　File No. _____-_____

　　　　　　　SURROGATE'S COURT — 　　COUNTY

CITATION
THE PEOPLE OF THE STATE OF NEW YORK,
By the Grace of God Free and Independent

TO

A petition having been duly filed by _____,
who is domiciled at _____

YOU ARE HEREBY CITED TO SHOW CAUSE before the Surrogate's Court, ____ County, at _____, _____, New York, on _____, at 9:30 o'clock in the forenoon of that day, why a decree should not be made in the estate of _____, lately domiciled at _____, admitting to probate a Will dated _____ [and Codicil(s) dated _____], a copy of which is attached, as the Will of _____ deceased, relating to real and personal property, and directing that

☐ Letters Testamentary issue to _____
☐ Letters of Trusteeship issue to _____
☐ Letters of Administration c.t.a. issue to _____

State any further relief requested

Dated, Attested and Sealed,　　　　　　　　　Hon. _____
　　　　　　　　　　　　　　　　　　　　　　　　　　　　　　　　　Surrogate
_____
　　　　　(Seal)　　　　　　　　　　　　　　_____
　　　　　　　　　　　　　　　　　　　　　　　　　　　　　　　　　Chief Clerk

Attorney for Petitioner _____ Tel. No. _____
Address of Attorney _____

[NOTE: This citation is served upon you as required by law. You are not required to appear. If you fail to appear it will be assumed you do not object to the relief requested. You have a right to have an attorney appear for you.]

Ch. 25　　PROBATE AND ESTATE ADMINISTRATION　§ 25.55

§ 25.55　Forms—Affidavit of Service of Citation

Form P-7 (7/99)

[Note: File Proof of Service at least 2 days before return date. State clearly date, time and place of service and name of person served. (Uniform Rule 207.7(c) [22 NYCRR])]

SURROGATE'S COURT OF THE STATE OF NEW YORK
COUNTY OF _____

Probate Proceeding, Will of

_____ Deceased.

AFFIDAVIT OF SERVICE OF CITATION

File No. _____ - _____

STATE OF _____
COUNTY OF _____ } ss.:

_____ of _____ being duly sworn, says, that I am over the age of eighteen years; that I made personal service of the citation herein dated _____, and a copy of the Will/Codicil on each person named below, each of whom deponent knew to be the person mentioned and described in said citation, by delivering to and leaving with each of them personally a true copy of said citation and Will/Codicil, as follows:

Name of person served _____
　Description: Sex _____ Color of skin _____ Color of hair _____
　　Approximate age _____ Weight _____ Height _____
　at _____ o'clock _____.m. on the _____ day of _____, _____
　at _____

Name of person served _____
　Description: Sex _____ Color of skin _____ Color of hair _____
　　Approximate age _____ Weight _____ Height _____
　at _____ o'clock _____.m. on the _____ day of _____, _____
　at _____

Name of person served _____
　Description: Sex _____ Color of skin _____ Color of hair _____
　　Approximate age _____ Weight _____ Height _____
　at _____ o'clock _____.m. on the _____ day of _____, _____
　at _____

　　That none of the aforesaid persons is in the military service as defined by the Act of Congress known as the "Soldiers' and Sailors' Civil Relief Act of 1940" and in the New York "Soldiers' and Sailors' Civil Relief Act."

_____
Signature

_____
Print Name

Sworn to before me this _____ day of
_____, _____

_____
Notary Public
(Affix Notary Stamp or Seal)

Name of Attorney _____ Tel. No. _____
Address of Attorney _____

§ 25.57 PROBATE AND ESTATE ADMINISTRATION   Ch. 25

§ 25.57 Forms—Waiver and Consent

Form P-4 (12/96)

SURROGATE'S COURT OF THE STATE OF NEW YORK
COUNTY OF

Probate Proceeding, Will of

_____ Deceased.

**WAIVER OF PROCESS;
CONSENT TO PROBATE**

File No. _____ -19_____

TO THE SURROGATE'S COURT, COUNTY OF KINGS

The undersigned, being of full age and sound mind, residing at the address written below and interested in this proceeding as set forth in paragraph 6a of the petition, hereby waives the issuance and service of citation in this matter and consents that the court admit to probate the decedent's Last Will and Testament dated _____ [and Codicil(s), if any, dated _____], a copy of each of which testamentary instrument has been received by me, and that

☐ Letters Testamentary issue to _____

☐ Letters of Trusteeship issue to _____
   of the following trusts: _____

_____   _____   _____   _____
Date   Signature   Street Address Relationship

               _____   _____
               Print Name   City/State/Zip

STATE OF
COUNTY OF   } ss.:

On _____, 19_____, before me personally appeared _____ to me known and known to me to be the person described in and who executed the foregoing waiver and consent and duly acknowledged the execution thereof.

_____
Notary Public
(Affix Notary Stamp or Seal)

Name of Attorney _____   Tel. No. _____
Address of Attorney _____

Ch. 25   PROBATE AND ESTATE ADMINISTRATION   § 25.58

§ 25.58 Forms—Notice of Probate

Form P-6 (12/96)

SURROGATE'S COURT OF THE STATE OF NEW YORK
COUNTY OF .

Probate Proceeding, Will of
Deceased.

NOTICE OF PROBATE
(SCPA 1409)

File No. _____ –19_____

NOTICE IS HEREBY GIVEN THAT:

1. The Will dated _____ [and Codicil(s) dated _____] of the above named decedent, domiciled at _____,
County of _____, New York,
has been / will be offered for probate in the Surrogate's Court for the County of Kings.

2. The name(s) of proponent(s) of said Will is/are _____,
whose address(es) is/are _____
_____.

3. The name and post office address of each person named or referred to in the petition who has not been served or has not appeared, or waived service of process, with a statement whether such person is named or referred to in the Will as legatee, devisee, trustee, guardian or substitute or successor executor, trustee or guardian, and as to any such person who is an infant or an incompetent, the name and post office address of a person upon whom service of process may be made on behalf of such infant or incompetent is as follows:

Name	Mailing Address	Nature of Interest or Status

(Use additional sheets if necessary)

Dated: _____, 19_____

[NOTE: Complete Affidavit of Mailing on reverse. If serving infant 14 years of age or older, list and mail to infant as well as parent or guardian.]

Name of Attorney _____ Tel. No. _____
Address of Attorney _____

AFFIDAVIT OF MAILING NOTICE OF PROBATE

STATE OF
COUNTY OF } ss.:

_____, residing at

_____,

being duly sworn, says that he/she is over the age of 18 years, that on the _____ day of _____, 19_____, he/she deposited in the post office or in a post office box regularly maintained by the government of the United States in the _____ of _____, State of New York, a copy of the foregoing Notice of Probate contained in a securely closed postpaid wrapper directed to each of the persons named in said Notice at the places set opposite their respective names.

_____
Signature

_____
Print Name

Sworn to before me this _____ day of _____, 19_____

_____
Notary Public
(Affix Notary Stamp or Seal)

Ch. 25   PROBATE AND ESTATE ADMINISTRATION   § 25.59

§ 25.59 Forms—Deposition Affidavit of Subscribing Witness

Form P-3 (8/99)

SURROGATE'S COURT OF THE STATE OF NEW YORK
COUNTY OF

Probate Proceeding, Will of

a

Deceased.

AFFIDAVIT OF ATTESTING WITNESS
(After Death)
Pursuant to SCPA 1406

File No. _____ - _____

STATE OF
COUNTY OF   } ss.:

The undersigned witness, being duly sworn, deposes and says:

(1) I have been shown (check one)
    ☐ the original instrument
    ☐ a court-certified photographic reproduction of the original instrument
dated _____, purporting to be [a Codicil to] the Last Will and Testament of the above-named decedent.

(2) On the date indicated in such instrument [and under the supervision of _____ _____, an attorney], I saw the decedent subscribe the same at the place where decedent's signature appears, and I heard the decedent declare such instrument to be [a Codicil to] his/her Last Will and Testament.

(3) I thereafter signed my name to such instrument as a witness thereto at the request of the decedent and in the presence of the decedent, and I saw the other witness(es), _____
_____
sign his/her/their name(s) at the end of such instrument as witness(es) thereto.

(4) At the time the decedent subscribed and executed such instrument, the decedent was, to the best of my knowledge and belief, upwards of 18 years of age, and in all respects appeared to be of sound and disposing mind, memory and understanding, competent to make a will, and not under any restraint.

(5) The decedent could read, write and converse in the English language, and was not suffering from defects of sight, hearing or speech, or any other physical or mental impairment which would affect his/her capacity to make a valid will. The purported instrument was the only copy of said [Codicil to the] Will executed on that occasion, and was not executed in counterparts.

(6) I am making this affidavit at the request of _____.

_____
Signature of Witness

_____
Print Name

_____
Street Address

_____
City/State/Zip

Sworn to before me this _____ day of
_____. _____

_____
Notary Public
(Affix Notary Stamp or Seal)

[NOTE: Each witness must be shown either the original will or a court-certified reproduction thereof. The notary public subscribing to this affidavit may not be a party or witness to the Will.]

§ 25.61 PROBATE AND ESTATE ADMINISTRATION   Ch. 25

§ 25.61 Forms—Decree Granting Probate

FORM 712

At a Surrogate's Court held in and for the County of
the   day of   , in the year one thousand nine hundred and

Present. Hon.   , Judge of the Surrogate's Court of
County

In the Matter of Proving
the Last Will and Testament of

File No. _____ 19____

Decree Granting Probate.

SATISFACTORY PROOF having been made that jurisdiction has been obtained of all persons entitled to notice of this proceeding.

And the witnesses to said Last Will and Testament   having been sworn and examined, their examination having been reduced to writing, and filed, and it appearing that said Will   duly executed, and that the Testat   , at the time of executing   , was in all respects competent to make a Will, and not under restraint; and this Court being satisfied of the genuineness of the Will   , and the validity of execution; and the Probate thereof not having been contested;

IT IS DECREED, that the instrument   offered for probate herein be, and the same hereby admitted to probate as the Last Will and Testament   of the said
                                                                                              deceased,
valid to pass Real and Personal property, and that the said Will and this Decree be recorded, and that Letters Testamentary be issued to the Execut who may qualify thereunder.

Chapter 26

PERSONAL INJURY

(updated in-house)

Table of Sections

26.21 Investigation—Automobile Accidents—Application of No–Fault
26.27 Claims Procedure for Automobile Accidents—Filing Notice of Claim with the Motor Vehicle Accident Indemnity Corporation—Procedure for Cases in Which There Is No Insurance
26.28 ___ ___ Procedure for Cases in Which There Is No Insurance and the Identity of the Wrongdoer Is Not Ascertainable (Hit and Run)
26.37 The Answer
26.42 Discovery—Generally
26.48 Settlement
26.49 Liens
26.52 Trial

Westlaw Electronic Research

See Westlaw Electronic Research Guide preceding the Summary of Contents.

---

§ 26.21 Investigation—Automobile Accidents—Application of No–Fault

PAGE 654:

[*Replace note 2 with the following.*]

2. 11 NYCRR § 65.11; No Fault Arbitration Decision 1781.

§ 26.27 Claims Procedure for Automobile Accidents—Filing Notice of Claim with the Motor Vehicle Accident Indemnity Corporation—Procedure for Cases in Which There Is No Insurance

PAGE 664:

[*Replace note 1 with the following.*]

1. Insurance Law § 5208(a)(1)(A–C).

§ 26.28 Claims Procedure for Automobile Accidents—Filing Notice of Claim with the Motor Vehicle Accident Indemnity Corporation—Procedure for Cases in Which There Is No Insurance and the Identity of the Wrongdoer Is Not Ascertainable (Hit and Run)

PAGE 665:

[*Replace note 2 with the following.*]

2. Insurance Law § 5208(a)(2)(A)(i-iii).

§ 26.37 The Answer

PAGE 675:

[*Replace note 1 with the following.*]

1. CPLR 3018.

§ 26.42 Discovery—Generally

PAGE 683:

[*The last sentence in the third-from-last paragraph on the page should read: "Note, however, that the information concerning the* **defendant's** *physical condition is not discoverable unless the defendant asserts the condition in a counterclaim.*[17]*"*]

[*Add to end of note 17.*]

17. *See also* Lopez v. Oquendo, ___ A.D.2d ___, 690 N.Y.S.2d 584 (1st Dep't 1999) (holding that "a litigant does not waive the physician-patient privilege merely by defending a personal injury action in which his or her mental or physical condition is in controversy unless the litigant 'affirmatively asserts the condition either by way of counterclaim or to excuse the conduct complained of by the plaintiff,'" quoting Koump v. Smith, 25 N.Y.2d 287, 294, 303 N.Y.S.2d 858, 861, 250 N.E.2d 857, 864 (1969)).

§ 26.48 Settlement

PAGE 688:

[*Delete footnote 2 and the reference to footnote 2 in the text.*]

§ 26.49 Liens

PAGE 689:

[*Replace note 2 with the following.*]

2. Social Services Law § 104–b.

[*Replace note 3 with the following.*]

3. Social Services Law § 104–b(2).

PAGE 690:

[*Replace note 4 with the following.*]

    4. Social Services Law § 104–b(3).

§ 26.52   Trial

PAGE 694:

[*Replace note 2 with the following.*]

    2. 22 NYCRR § 202.42(d).